The Fence Jumper

BY THE SAME AUTHOR

Love at First Flight (with Charles Spalding)

When the Bough Breaks

Yesterday's Hero

Good Friday 1963

The Paper Bullet

New Lease on Life

Welcome Back, Billy Rawls

Chihuahua 1916

The Fence Jumper

A Search for the Greener Pasture

OTIS CARNEY

Green Hill Publishers, Inc.
Ottawa, Illinois

10 9 8 7 6 5 4 3 2 1

Copyright © 1983 by John Otis Carney

Printed in the United States of America

Copies of this book may be purchased from the publisher for $13.95. All inquiries and catalogue requests should be addressed to Green Hill Publishers, Inc. 722 Columbus Street, Ottawa, IL 61350. (815) 434-7905

ISBN: 0-89803-131-1

Library of Congress Cataloging in Publication Data

Carney, Otis.
    The fence jumper.

    1. Carney, Otis.   2. United States--Biography.
3. Ranch life--West (U.S.) I. Title.
CT275.C3125A33 1983   978'.09'94   83-16308
ISBN 0-89803-131-1

*He maketh me to lie down in green pastures:
he leadeth me beside the still waters.*

Psalm 23

*We must be still and still moving
Into another intensity
For a further union, a deeper communion
Through the dark cold and the empty desolation,
The wave cry, the wind cry, the vast waters
Of the petrel and the porpoise. In my end
is my beginning.*

*T.S. Eliot
Four Quartets*

Contents

Introduction   1

1 Spring of the Okies   5

2 Summer of the Elk   33

3 Fall of the Masked Bobwhite   65

4 Winter of the Moose   101

5 Summer of the Golden Trout   123

6 Ending the Beginning   211

Introduction

Twenty years ago, my wife Teddy and I and our three sons left Los Angeles and moved to a cattle ranch in Wyoming.

We didn't know much about ranching, but in our youth and dreams were convinced we could learn. Because I'd still be pursuing my career as a writer, we hoped that our uprooting would be no more harrowing than, say, changing job locales from Chicago to New York.

Once we realized how much we loved the freedom of our new life, we doubled our bet and bought a second ranch, this one in Arizona, near the Mexican border. Now we had two beautiful pieces of land, cows for Teddy to milk north and south, and chickens, calves, colts, and bird dogs at both ends. Running two ranches over a thousand miles apart, and running between them, led to many an exhausted night. Teddy and I would glance at each other and say, we've got to be out of our minds to be doing this! Yet by the time dawn had broken over the snow-capped Wind Rivers of Wyoming or the coppery Cerro Colorado in Arizona, it was blessings, not woes, we were counting, and thanking God for them.

Now, they certainly didn't add up to anything in dollars. You can't put a price tag on the flash of a trout in a stream. Or on the patient smile of an old horse when he realized you had lost the way, and only he knew how to get you home. And yet, when we began dimly to grasp the meaning of such things, it was because we were seeing them with new eyes.

This was the shock.

We hadn't just moved to a different geography. We were having to move out of ourselves. Jumping the old fence into the new pasture—that was the easy part, simply a physical leap. But learning to live with it after we got there—that was the slow and often painful transition. We had to develop a different mind-set, learn to think and react in new ways—many of them perilous because they warred against the value systems and rigid codes of our former lives. Old, crusted habits die hard; it took years to replace them with humbler treasures. And if these glittered at all, like fool's gold, it was because we'd wept for them in our comedies of errors, shattered hopes, and, more often, our joys.

So that's the story I want to leave under my rock, somewhere on this trail west, for the next searchers who'll be following us. I hope they'll learn more quickly than I did that this land out here, in its majesty and simplicity, can only inspire a man to the greener pasture. But whether we can change ourselves to find it is perhaps like the elusive still waters that lie far up a distant canyon. Some days we can see them clearly; others, not at all. So, the next day, we get up and try to reach them again. There's only the trying. That's what jumping the fence is all about.

OTIS CARNEY
Cora, Wyoming

1

Spring of the Okies

That April afternoon in Arizona the desert lay hot and still: even benign. There was no wind, which normally blew in the spring. Visibility was unlimited. From our bedroom in the old Las Delicias adobe, I could see the sweep of the Altar Valley, nineteen square miles that we owned and leased, a sea of mesquite, greening now, and the buttery cactus flowers beginning to bloom. Further east rose the red cliffs of the Cerro Colorado, and beyond them, the towering bluish mountains of the Santa Ritas, running down to the Mexican border.

That was the run we'd be making in a few moments: a two-hour drive to Nogales, Old Mexico, where my wife

Teddy and I would go to a party with old friends. We'd discovered many former acquaintances scattered around the Tucson area. But when one lived eight miles from his nearest neighbor, as we did on the Las Delicias, he could hardly be called a social butterfly. On the other hand, I was comforted to know that I was able to get out and into the action if I wanted to, a far cry from our ranch in Wyoming where we would have to ski four miles to our car, find it frozen in a snowbank, and then, if we managed to get it started, where?

So I was pleased as I stood in our bedroom, dressing for the party ahead. There still seemed something awfully comfortable in slipping on the familiar gray flannels, loafers, and a seersucker coat. And a delight in seeing Teddy so willowy in her new Mexican white lace dress, her brown hair spilling over the high collar. The Nogales parties were always filled with pretty Mexican girls, mariachis strumming around, and margaritas that never seemed to go dry. I was looking forward to many *gran bailes* with Teddy that night. In short, it was a long way from the corral, and we needed such a change right then.

We'd been working hard getting ourselves settled on the Las Delicias. It's always difficult when you take over a new piece of land. You have to get the feel of it and absorb the inevitable surprises that the real estate salesmen either don't know or don't want you to. As a neighbor said to me after I'd been on the ranch a few months: "Son, if you can run cows in this burroweed desert you can run 'em anyplace in the world." That was the same neighbor who used to frown bleakly at the sky and add: "Wal, you can say this much: every day she don't rain is just one day closer to when she does."

But, in a counting of blessings, as Teddy and I drove through the ranch courtyard, we did seem to have several things going for us. With the Las Delicias, I'd inherited a foreman named Faustino. He spoke only Spanish, but I regarded this as a chance to improve my own. And what a happy, simpatico little fellow he was. As we passed his adobe, which was close to ours and shaded under an ancient tamarack, I could see Faustino's children hunched beside the blue glow of the TV. His wife was industriously sweeping the dirt yard, which Mexican women always do. Faustino, I'd convinced myself, knew where the bodies had been buried from the old mistakes on the ranch. He could fix pipelines when they leaked, and track wild cattle which we had to gather out of the cactus-filled canyons of the Baboquivari Mountains. Actually, the former owner had used Faustino as a "second man," but because I was determined to run a no-frills outfit and could afford only a one-man show, I immediately promoted Faustino to *mayordomo.*

His reaction had struck me as curious at the time. He burst into giggles of astonishment. I assumed he was delighted. After a few months of watching him work, I could see that he was an outstanding roper. Often, he did seem a little hesitant during our roundups, as if waiting for me to tell him what to do. But no matter. He'd grow with the job, and I was so new at a desert cattle operation I felt I should learn the hard knocks firsthand anyway.

A few doubts did gnaw at me, however. Faustino, like many vaqueros raised in southern Mexico, had not seen much machinery in his lifetime. He drove tractors after only a sketchy servicing, and trucks always too fast. The fact that he claimed not to know how to shoe a horse annoyed me somewhat, but I avoided a showdown by hiring a neighbor to do it, probably better, and we simply forged ahead. There was no time to look back, because we'd just begun a big yearling program on the ranch.

When I bought the Las Delicias, the feedlot that came with the place was a wasteland of ugly steel corrals and sun shades that thrummed in the wind. I regarded the entire thing as a white elephant, crusted over with tumbleweed.

But soon I was approached by a local cowman, a pleasant young fellow who smoked cheroots and wore an Arizona straw hat jammed down over his sun-squinted eyes. No question but that he was honest, and when he proposed to me that we joint-venture on runnng yearling cattle in the feedlot and on our Wyoming grass, I thought it sounded like the best game in town: a money machine for a literary man who, anyway, really had to get back to his typewriter right then.

Now I'd learned in previous years a good bit about shuttling yearling cattle between Mexico and Wyoming. After all, that had been the primary economic reason for buying Las Delicias. To ensure that we'd always have an adequate supply of Mexican cattle, and at the right price, I had set up my own *negocio* with friends in Sonora. These were mysterious fellows you could never get on the telephone, and had to dine with no earlier than 11 P.M. We'd meet in shadowy cantinas in hamlets named after forgotten martyrs, and would scribble our price computations on soggy beer napkins. I spent days drifting around remote mountain haciendas, rarely seeing the cattle I was buying, but taking them solely on trust. Strangely, the system worked. The cattle I ended up with were always quite good and properly cheap when I crossed them at Sasabe, and trundled them the twenty-two miles to the Las Delicias.

Thus, I was disappointed when my new podner in the feedlot venture had shaken his head: "Naw, Otis, these common Mexican corrientes just ain't gonna do for us now. We gotta have quality, volume—and the only place we'll get it is from my source down in Georgia."

I didn't know they even *had* cattle in Georgia. "Hell yes," my podner assured me. "Mississippi, Alabama, too; all them swamps. That's where the numbers are. The Okies got 'em in their backyards—is why they call 'em Okies. And my source can bundle them little buggers in here, a truckload a day if we want it, every one the same size and shape, i-dentical good do-ers. That's got to beat you running around in Sonora, yammering Tex-Mex and dealing with people we can't never trust."

Perhaps it did make sense. After all, he was the cowman in the outfit. And anyway, what I'd been doing, my Tex-Mexing down there, drinking cerveza, seemed but marking time while my writing was going slowly. Now I could get back to my typewriter and leave the numbers to him. As he'd chuckled over our ledgers: "Hell, Otis, this is no big thing. So far, we ain't got but a quarter of a million dollars in it. And that's one hundred percent borrowed!" What better security could a man have than several thousand steers, galloping into a sensational market?

On the strength of such optimism, Teddy and I drove out the ranch road that April afternoon. Ahead of us, the sunset was beginning to enflame the Cerro Colorado, and closer, the black shapes I could see, grazing out in the mesquite, were our first Okie steers, filling their bellies here until we were ready to ship the choicest ones to Wyoming, and sell the others locally.

Beside me, Teddy switched on the air-conditioner so that our four miles of ranch road wouldn't dust up her party dress. And with good reason, because racing toward us now was a truck and cattle trailer, billowing out a great sandy cloud. As it came closer, its windshield glinting in the sun, I recognized Faustino, driving too fast as usual. But he slowed at our approach and waved happily. In his delighted Spanish, he jerked his thumb at the enormous trailer and cried that his cargo was: "Muy buen bunchee, Señor, muy gordo, very fat...!" Bring us a bunchee dinero when we'd sell them tomorrow, verdad? Then the trailer swept past in a kind of thunderous rattling that I imagine delights a factory owner when he feels the throbbing of his machines, pumping out dollars. A moment later, Teddy said, "Darling, is that a steer lying in the road?"

I braked the stationwagon. There on a dusty bend in the shade of mesquite lay a sleek-fat Okie. He was simply resting in the shadows; no doubt we'd missed him on our roundup. I beeped my horn at him and chuckled, thinking, don't worry, smarty, we'll get you tomorrow. Only he didn't move. I beeped a second time. Teddy said, "What's a steer doing lying in the road?"

What he was doing was trying to get up on three broken legs. "Oh, God," Teddy cried. "Look!" We both lunged out of the car, sluffing unbelievingly through the dust, loafers, Spanish lace, and all. Now we could hear the bleating and wailing. Just beyond the turn and sharp dip of an arroyo lay a battlefield strewn with black lumps, sprawled grotesquely, shattered bones, internal injuries. Two hundred dollars a head was what they'd bring tomorrow, and not one would live to go to the sale! Teddy was on her knees beside a steer, clutching his head. I simply stomped and cursed. Faustino! That child, that idiot! And I a bigger one for deluding myself that he could run a ranch. In his hurry to get home to watch TV's Bugs Bunny with his kids, he'd careened into the arroyo, ripped off the trailer door, and shelled out twenty-five of our best steers like peas from a pod.

"Faustino!" I groaned moments later at his house. "Didn't you *feel* the trailer getting lighter...that *something* was happening in the back end?" It was a broad concept to express in my kitchen Spanish, but Faustino kept shrugging with nervous little giggles. No sabe, señor, just something in the hands of God, verdad? And anyway, I should look at the bright side: at least the whole bunchee didn't fall out. Mira! Three steers were standing fat and happy in the corral!

With the TV cartoons yapping in Faustino's kitchen, I felt that his rope had just taken a dally around my heart.

Well, I couldn't run from it anymore. As little "Hunior"—Junior—his baby, trundled on his red tin kiddycar, and his wife and girls peeped their black eyes around the kitchen door, I began the process of firing Faustino.

And that, given the closeness of our lives on the ranch, made it sticky business trying to drive the prodigal out. I'm also very poor at it. It took a week of having nightly "wheeskies" with Faustino before I could make him understand that he had to go. As an added complication, his wife, children, and then Teddy came down with a racking flu. In what I thought was a noble gesture, Faustino drove Teddy and his family to the Mexican clinic in Sasabe, where they all received a healthy gamma globulin shot. At length, I located for Faustino an even higher-paying job over in what he called "Juma." On this Yuma, Arizona, irrigated farm, he could drive tractors around with many other fellows and hence remain inconspicuous.

On the final day, Faustino loaded our trailer with all his belongings, including beds, furniture, and Hunior's little red kiddycar we'd given him. Down the ranch road they went, Faustino waving at us gaily, leaving me astounded that he could be smiling in such a moment. Little did I realize that the joke was already on me!

La vida mejor ("the better life"), they called it, and in its pursuit, wetbacks from Mexico would come streaming across the Las Delicias, particularly in the farming months of spring.

When I'd be riding down in the desert flatlands, I'd often bump into two or three compadres napping under a mesquite, or others skittering across the open hardpans. They'd be glancing nervously at the sky, hoping the droning Border Patrol Cessna wouldn't spot them and radio their location to the wandering green jeeps. In these vehicles the patrolmen regularly swept our arroyos with rugs made of old tires. When wetbacks crossed the sand, they'd leave fresh footprints and the patrolmen could snare them, somewhere up the long track to the better life.

A sad and courageous track, really. Unless you've lived on the border, you can't know the desperation in it. Many of the wetbacks who came footsore and hollow-eyed into the patio of our house had walked over a thousand miles to get there. In Mexico their families were too big, too hungry, and underemployed. These lithe youths, some in their early teens, were regarded as their hope and sole support. Though we were clearly not farmers or even potential employers, the Las Delicias must have been on the mental maps of legions of wetbacks over the generations. Through word of mouth it seemed to be regarded as a safe place, and thus some Jose or Jaime would appear at our kitchen door, accompanied by a group of compañeros who'd be squatting a respectful distance away under the shade of a palo verde. The spokesman would usually beg *comida* first, and then offer to work free, just for the food. Once in a while, when we had trails to chop in the mesquite, or some unwanted job like building fence up through the rocks, we'd hire a boy or two. They preferred working in pairs, so they weren't lonely. But normally I'd just tell them that ours was a "rancho de ganado, no trabajo—y muy pobre." Very poor. They'd grin at that, as if to say, Do you know how lucky you are, patron? Then Teddy would start rooting around the kitchen for apples, frijoles, tortillas. In the season when the migrants were the thickest, she even began brewing up a mixture of nuts, raisins, sesame seeds, and granola—what the mountain climbers call "gorp," and with it she put the wetbacks on a health-food kick. So much so that at times I'd find some of them sleeping it off in distant arroyos, their bellies puffed up from processing this unaccustomed dose of protein.

We had all kinds of wetbacks: the halt, the lame, and

the nutty, too. One poor fellow was a drooler; I assumed either a drug addict or a mental patient, and I did advise the Border Patrol that it ought to pick him up and get him medical attention. We also had raconteurs, who would tell us stories of "cuevas ricas," caves laden with gold that they'd stumbled on in the brooding Baboquivari canyons behind our ranch house. The logical question was: If these old-Spanish-Indian treasure troves were so rich, what was Mario or Pepe doing here begging for work? Ah, but, Señor, they'd grin, it was at night when he'd found the cave and, Dios *mio!* for the life of him he could not now remember its exact location. Then, too, there was the terrible problem of *leones*, mountain lions prowling the Baboquivaris. Did I not know that such and such hombre from Zacatecas was eaten by a lion in the canyons above us, his compañeros finding only his hat and shoes?

Lore and lies. Promise and piety. They were a mixture of all such things, the wetbacks we came to know. And their migration, their restlessness, was not only to fill their own bellies and those of their families at home, but to give them a chance to see those things the magazines and television showed them were the commonplace riches of America. One wetback who worked a few days in Teddy's vegetable garden used to glance often into the house. He'd point at a chair, stove, or lamp, always with the same question: "Que costo?" ("How much does that cost?") How many hours, laboring in some Phoenix lettuce field? How many thousand dream miles away?

Yet, for other wetbacks, there were deeper desires. One, who stayed a week or so, wanted to exchange some of his salary for the child's watercolor kit he'd seen me dabbling with. I gave it to him. After a hard day's work, instead of sleeping, he'd be sitting out in the wetback adobe under a naked light bulb, painting primitive scenes of his native land. Shortly before he left, he approached me and said, in shy earnestness: "Was the patron aware that his Las Delicias ranch did not have a cross?"

Well, frankly, no. I hadn't given it any thought.

He shook his head. "In Mexico, señor, all ranchos must have a cross, so that travelers will know it is a safe and blessed place."

"Ah." I nodded and stood instructed, never realizing that he'd spend the next day, Sunday, his day off, hammering out and painting a six-foot gleaming white crucifix, which he then could lug on his back and plant atop a rocky hill where it could overlook the entire ranch.

My city friends insist that we were exploiting the wetbacks. I wonder. Might it not have been that we were learning from them treasured ways of life that we'd forgotten for too long? Perhaps that's why I don't have any glib solution for the problem of "illegal immigration," and am not sure that the politicians or labor unions do either. All I know is that the wetbacks who crossed my path seemed to operate on a different set of values from mine, or those that I could expect to find in the usual American ranch workers. To be sure, there were lazy wetbacks, corner cutters, and chronic gripers. But deep in them, arising from somewhere out of their smoky pasts, dwelt an ingrained dignity and a sense of responsibility about their work. "Mi responsibilidad," they'd say with pride, as if their usually crude hand labor were a blessed thing and they were eager to accept the sweat of its toil. Whether they ever reached their *vida mejor*, they seemed content to leave the outcome in *los manos de Dios*, as long as their hands did their part. When we finally paid them off, they'd hitch their plastic water bottles and serapes up over their shoulders, and trudge on toward the next chance, north.

Occasionally, some city friend of ours, visiting the ranch, would gasp at the unexpected sight of a wetback face, peering in the window. "But aren't you afraid," the visitor would ask, "that they'd come in and rob you? Even kill you?"

My usual answer was that I'd be more afraid in Tucson or New York, and probably least of all down in some pueblo in Mexico! In a restaurant in one such place, Teddy had once left her purse overnight, having forgotten it. After a sleepless night we raced back in the morning. In the purse was a diamond ring that had been in Teddy's family from pre–Civil War days. Unfound by the Yankee looters, the ring had financed Teddy's grandfather through medical school. At the restaurant a shy little Mexican waitress presented the purse to Teddy. Not only was the ring still there, but also several hundred dollars in cash—untouched. In all the years that wetbacks crossed the Las Delicias, I never missed so much as a screwdriver.

They were a different breed all right, and that's why, in the spring that Faustino left us, we had such hopes for a young wetback girl who came into our lives. It was a coincidence, as in an act of God, and couldn't have happened at a better time. One of her brothers, who'd wandered in one day from Sonora and was cutting mesquite for us, happened to notice that we had a yawning vacancy in the kitchen; that is, nobody. In the isolation of a ranch, help is almost impossible to get, and that includes cleaning women, babysitters, and most of all, plumbers. You do it yourself. And Teddy had been doing it for quite a few months when the young wetback returned with his older sister. Her name was Refugia, a hardy girl of twenty whose face showed a classic serenity. Refugia's brother called her *muy seria*, and little wonder she was serious about finding *la vida mejor*. She'd grown up in a two-room adobe with a gaggle of brothers and sisters. When their father had died, their mother had simply shooed them out and told them, *Andale!* Walk, or starve. After watching Refugia whisk gracefully and efficiently around the kitchen, we hoped she'd stay with us forever. With her mopping, sweeping, and humming Mexican ranchera songs, she made the rambling old adobe glisten, and

Teddy was overjoyed. While the brother was sawing our winter firewood supply, Refugia was helping Teddy pack for our annual summer migration to Wyoming.

Then one morning, a few weeks after Faustino had gone happily down the road, up the road came a green sedan. As I lazed out of the kitchen, I recognized the clean-cut faces and Smokey the Bear campaign hats of two Border Patrolmen. Nothing unusual about this. They were always prowling around the ranch, looking for drug smugglers. I considered them friends, fine young men. "Hello, fellas," I said. "How about a cup of coffee?"

"Well, thanks, Mr. Carney, but we'll have to take a raincheck today. We're here for your wetbacks."

As I stood there gulping, one athletic young agent dashed out of the sedan to the screaming bandsaw and collared Refugia's woodcutting brother. The other agent said, smiling: "Now, if you could bring out that boy's sister. You know, the one who's been working for Mrs. Carney in the house."

Of course I knew! But did *they* have to? Lord, I thought, what kind of radar were they using? For years now, they'd driven up the ranch road looking for tracks, but rarely had come into the house enclosure. Perhaps they felt we needed all the help we could get, and besides, these Sonoran field hands weren't the types who'd disappear into the interior of the country. But something had clearly changed now. When Teddy started to protest, I told her we couldn't harbor wetbacks, so give up, run another ad in the Tucson paper.

Teddy and Refugia wrapped around each other, sobbing. Bits and pieces of Refugia's humble wardrobe and plastic curlers began coming out of her room in paper bags. Even the patient Border Patrolmen helped, carrying shoes and a dress on a hanger. Teddy sniffled and pressed dollars into the prisoner's hands. Then the steel cage in the back of the sedan clicked shut. It seemed rather crowded, I noticed; Refugia and her brother were stuffed beside two other Mexicans in the back seat. One of these seemed to be signaling to me, putting his finger to his lips. "Oh, yes, Mr. Carney," the patrolman said, "we also picked up your other two boys...you know, the ones working on that ranch you lease."

I seemed to be quite a wetback industry, and began hemming, "Oh, *that* ranch!" Well, it had no connection with me, of course. My partner in the feedlot rented it; he had to, because of all the cattle we now owned.

The patrolmen just smiled, as if to say, that's your problem. And when they wheeled off, our little Sonora family, unlike Faustino's, didn't wave at us all the way down the road. They wept.

It was a scene that might well have played on "As the World Turns," but this, unfortunately, was real world, and the Big Scriptwriter was not done with us yet. He hadn't figured on the vengeance of a woman scorned.

"They're not getting away with it," Teddy gritted tearfully. No Border Patrol was going to wreck her household, particularly when everybody in Tucson worked wetbacks; it wasn't against the law. What we were jolly well going to do, Teddy informed me—she'd already whispered it to Refugia in the tearful parting—we'd simply buzz down to Nogales Saturday night, and smuggle Refugia home!

Absolutely not! I cried. That was *transporting*, punishable by fine or prison or both. "Don't be ridiculous!" Teddy scoffed. What with all the patrolmen had to do, chasing drug smugglers and really horrible people, did I think they'd bother with one poor little kitchen girl?

Of course they'd bother. That's what they were paid for. Then Teddy gripped my hands and began misting up. So I was going to abandon her in this big house, was that the idea? A second ranch she'd never wanted; would have to do everything alone, close the house in a month or so and open the other barn in Wyoming. She didn't quite say that it was Refugia or me, but we were getting there.

All right, dammit. Saturday night, then. Make the snatch.

The plot was ridiculously simple. Any Border Patrol-man could have figured it out. All Refugia had to do was cross through the gate at Nogales by showing her Mexican passport and giving the standard explanation that she was going shopping on the American side. Thousands did it daily. (Refugia had slipped her passport into Teddy's pocket so the patrolmen wouldn't confiscate it, and conspirator Teddy could later mail it to her.) Refugia would proceed fifty yards to the Safeway supermarket, buy a couple of chilis, and pop them into her brown paper bag. We, then, would idle across the shadowy Safeway parking lot, slither her into our car, and zoom off. Teddy had even planned an additional demonic cover for us. Instead of racing up the freeway as an amateur smuggler might, and run smack into a Border Patrol roadblock, we would be at a party with our fancy Nogales friends. That meant dinner at 10 P.M., the customary swim of margaritas, and rock dancing until all self-respecting Border Patrolmen would be long in bed.

Great. But just to thicken the plot, I did slip my .38 Police Positive into our glove compartment. That was for our two-hour sneak over the loneliest road in Arizona, known as the Arivaca cutoff, and frequented mainly by drug smugglers. I wanted to be packing iron, in case I ran into one of them, the really bad guys. Teddy just kept laughing. "You're such a square. You and your guilty conscience. Nothing's going to happen!"

As they say in the smuggling thrillers, it was a piece of cake, a beautiful desert night of stars; we never saw a light or passed anyone on the twisting loneliness of the Arivaca road. Refugia was sleeping peacefully in the back seat, and at 2 A.M., when we finally struck our Altar Valley road, I began floorboarding it, cattle guards rattling at me—thirteen, ten, five miles from the ranch now.

Teddy yawned luxuriantly. "See? See? All your worrying..."

What I was seeing at that moment was a tiny light, far behind, somewhere near the border. At this hour it could hardly be a tourist—probably just young Mexican lovers, necking as they drove. Anyhow, I stepped it up from seventy miles per hour to a more comfortable eighty-five.

A faint coyote howl mourned in the night. Coyote? With red blinking lights, hurtling behind me at the speed of sound! Teddy gripped my leg. "What...is it?"

She knew perfectly well what! They were in my mirror now, Smokey the Bear hats, siren screaming, lights wobbling, and I punching the brake and burning rubber. Maybe they were just trying to pass? Pass hell! They were jamming me off the road!

Teddy was pushing Refugia down in the back seat, hiding her under a coat. "What are we going to do?" she cried.

In some flee or fight mechanism, I was flinging open the door, charging like a wounded bull at the Border Patrol car, which had also lurched to a stop. In the normal greeting of these parts, two agents were standing flat-footed, their 12-gauge riot guns aimed at my throat. Identification friend or foe. In sheer self-defense I managed to croak out: "Fellas? Hey, dammit, you know *me!*" Name, rank, serial number, remember? The guy who lives on the Las Delicias?

The Border Patrolmen glanced at each other and sheepishly lowered the artillery. Wal sure, they grinned. They'd *thought* it was me—now they could recognize the car—but it was so late and there was supposed to be a drug intercept someplace up the road. Anyhow, they were really sorry for bothering me. If I'd just pull over and let them pass, they'd get that druggie who must be up ahead.

The last we saw of them were flashing lights, streaking north to where the real criminals were. "We did it!" Teddy cried, she and Refugia hugging again in a spray of rosary beads, and we were all home safe for life.

Monday afternoon I drove four miles down from the ranch house to get the mail. Our box stands beside the country road, not far from the site of our brush with justice. Well, I could smile about it now. Just a funny story. I opened the mail box. The top letter had an unfamiliar return address: "United States Attorney, Tucson."

Dear Mr. Carney,

It has come to the attention of this office that for some period of time, you have been engaged in the working and transporting of illegal aliens, not only here in Arizona but to your other ranch in Wyoming. We are hereby informing you...criminal offense...$10,000 fine...two years imprisonment... prosecute you...fullest extent of the law...

If I seemed to be skimming the letter, it was only that I was reading it, clutched on the steering wheel as I drove wildly back to the ranch house. See! See! I kept shouting at Teddy. So nobody cared, huh? We put it over on 'em? Then how come the U.S. attorney already *knew* we had transported a wetback into our house? Common criminals! All because some closets had to be cleaned!

"Ask your lawyer what to do," Teddy said, and thrust the phone at me.

I froze. "Don't touch it! They've bugged us!"

"Oh, come on. For one little kitchen girl?"

"For one big mistake," I cried. "You talked about it!" That Sunday afternoon, Teddy had telephoned her mother, then her sister, and gushed out every detail of the snatch and escape. No wonder they'd nailed us! They were wise to us all the time!

"Darling," Teddy said wearily. "If I talked on the phone late yesterday, and they heard, how would we get a letter in today's mail? Does any government bureau work that fast, or on Sunday?"

Well, I grudged, ... well, maybe not. But still I went stalking around the kitchen: Teddy's fault, conning me into this mess. Because now we were trapped, had the hot goods in the house, and if the Border Patrolmen drove up and asked for Refugia, we couldn't harbor. Then they would ask Refugia: How did you get here, señorita? And she'd be terrified into telling them. Transporting eh? Too bad, Mr. Carney. Where, I puzzled, would they send me? Leavenworth? Or out with the Watergate bunch at sun-baked Florence, so I could be closer to my second home?

I began lashing around for lawyers. My own was off on some carefree holiday, so finally I threw myself at the feet of a total stranger: pleasant young man in a bolo tie. Not wanting to discuss it on the phone (his advice), I raced the fifty miles to Tucson, met him in a parking lot where they couldn't possibly bug us. "Wal," he said, "sort of a pickle, isn't it?" Then he added that by no means should Teddy and I take the girl anyplace in a car. Possibly, he suggested, we could fob her off on someone so clean the Border Patrol would never stop him—say, a humble priest or doctor en route to minister to the sick in Mexico.

Well, we were out of doctors and priests right then, but we surely could have used one. By the time I got home, Refugia had come down with a raging flu. Now we'd have days of convalescence, trying to hide her in her room ten feet from where the Border Patrol had parked in its original seizure. I'd made up my mind: the moment Refugia was well enough to travel, she was going to pick up her shopping bag and *walk* back to the border. Young, strong thing, she could manage to do it, if it would keep me out of the slammer.

How could I even suggest that! Teddy cried. Perfectly inhuman! If the girl had to walk, she'd walk with her! At that moment there was a rapping on the screen door. I froze, catching a glimpse of a uniform. Then a voice barked, "Hey, is somebody in here ready to go to jail?"

Har-har-har. It was Teddy's brother, Bill Kent, strolling in to pick up his luncheon beer. The horrifying uniform I'd seen was only his faded Marine Corps dungarees that appeared unwashed since his days as a combat rifleman in Vietnam.

If there was ever time for a hero, my young brother-in-law was it. A rugged kid with soldier-of-fortune tendencies, he'd come out to help us with the feedlot, a form of rest and rehabilitation that he said was okay, but he sure missed the action in Nam.

No more, young Horatio. I just happen to have a little mission here. As I ticked off what I hoped he would do, Bill's eyes gleamed. Nothing to it. He'd bundle Refugia into his crummy, unsuspicious car, slip her over the Arivaca cutoff to Nogales; avoid contact with any human. If apprehended, he'd take the full blame himself, say she was his girlfriend. No connection with any Carney. Most important, once he had dumped her back into Old Mexico, he'd get on the telephone and release me from my anguish. Got it?

"Got it." Bill chuckled, exposing his missing tooth somebody had knocked out in a recent fight. "A last thing, skipper. How about a suicide pill?"

Har-har. I could have used one myself the next day. As Bill loaded Refugia into his junker and they roared off, I began pacing around the kitchen, counting the hours. Finally Teddy told me to go ride a horse someplace. I selected our remotest canyon, known as Diablo, and climbed thousands of feet up into the rocky crags where they couldn't possibly find me. Because, by then, I was certain I'd picked the wrong man. Bill was clearly unsuited by temperament for a sensitive mission like this. During his brief rehab on the ranch, including back-breaking work at the feedlot which we hoped would hone him down, something was still missing. The army of North Vietnam, of course. With no visible enemy, he simple vented himself on the nearest Customs officer or Border Patrolman. Whenever he'd come back from prowling the cantinas in Sasabe, Sonora, he insisted on picking fights with our normally benign Customs men, leaving them no choice but to tear apart his car, looking for drugs he didn't use. One peaceful evening, two Border Patrolmen screamed up our driveway after him, insisting he open his trunk. Teddy and I were out for a walk, interceding for a rubber-legged Bill, Teddy saying, "But please, officer. He's my brother." Then, "Oh, Bill, just open the damn trunk!" We were sure he had a body in there, the way he blank-blanked those blanking mothers. Of course, the trunk was finally opened and proved clean. Bill said you had to do that to the jarheads every so often, square 'em away so they wouldn't tromp on you.

A good six hours after the resmuggling had begun—I'd long been back in the house and was clutching a bourbon—the telephone rang. Collect, from Nogales. That would be Customs all right, even the final indignity of making me pay for the call. Yes, I sighed, I'd accept all charges.

The answer was a margarita-laden guffaw. Mission impossible complete. Then why the hell, I bellowed, had he waited so long to call me?

"Couple of little combat snafus," he chuckled.

"Like what?"

"Tell you when I get home."

Only he didn't make it home. About midnight, another collect call came from a lonely ranch to the south of us. No big thing, Bill grunted. He'd just caught some loose sand on the Arivaca road, spun in and ripped off a wheel. How about me coming to get him?

As we drove home in the ranch truck, not a Border Patrol light could be seen. First thing that happened, Bill said, after he'd picked up Refugia at our house, he realized he'd forgotten his wallet. That meant he had to turn back and go to the ranch feedlot where his wallet was in his trailer. Border Patrolmen cruised by the feedlot every day—sure enough, there they were. And whaddya know? With Refugia sitting big as life in the front seat, the patrolmen just drove right past and waved at their old trunk buddy, Bill.

Then, out on the Arivaca road, where there's never anyone, what did he do but run into a roadblock, game wardens and sheriffs stopping all cars and looking for javelina pigs, which were in season then. Why sure, fellas; Bill just opened the trunk for them and they waved him through. He had to stop again several times on the Nogales freeway, poor Refugia feeling a little car sick by then, so he walked her up and down the divider, in plain sight of two Border Patrol cars that cruised past. Nobody said a thing; he just slipped her across the line and bought her a big farewell dinner. It was only when he came back to the U.S. side—his face darkened now—those Customs goons hassled him, reached into his car, and said, "Hey, bud, watcha doin' carrying marijuana seeds?"

A pretty good fight erupted out of that one, Bill telling them where they could put their marijuana. He never smoked it; they'd just planted it on him. Entrapment. Okay, wise guy—they hauled him out of the car, stripped it, pulled the seats, air cleaner. Bill bared his missing tooth, grinning: "And do you know all they found?"

"I can't wait," I sighed. "What, Bill?"

"That pop gun in the glove compartment. Your .38 Police Positive."

"But it was in *my* car!" I echoed.

"Naw. You told me to take it, remember?... in case I had trouble on the Arivaca road."

"What did they say about the gun?" I was almost whispering now.

No big thing, he shrugged. They hassled him for carrying it without a permit, but he got off by telling the truth. It wasn't his gun... belonged to his brother-in-law. And where, they asked, was that man? Bill simply gave my full name and address. "Relax," he chuckled. "Dumb as those government clowns are, they could never put it together with your wetback business!"

Only twice, so far. There was always tomorrow.

About a week later, when my lawyer returned from vacation, I told him the whole story. He sniffed lawyer-ishly and said he'd check into it. When he called back in a couple of hours, sounding as if he were speaking from a bug-free parking lot, he said: "I'm not at liberty to tell you where I got this, but... did you ever have a foreman named Faustino?"

"Sure. I just fired him."

"How long ago?"

"About a month."

"Well, the joke's on you," the lawyer said, but he did the laughing. "This Faustino must have been a pretty shrewd cookie. Apparently when you fired him he called the Border Patrol and described in flowery detail all the wetbacks you were working, and how over the years you'd been hauling them up to Wyoming."

"That's a damn lie! We'd never..."

"The Border Patrol didn't believe it either. That's why they gave you several more weeks with your help. In fact, they were reluctant to pick them up at all, but they had to because they'd been informed on."

"Faustino?" I echoed. All the beds and therapy and Hunior's kiddycar. No wonder he left so happily. He had been paid the standard ten-dollar-a-head Judas fee for each wetback he turned in... and he once a wetback himself!

Well, amigo, I thought, you got even, didn't you? I

could imagine him giggling over at Juma, remembering how he'd dumped the señor's new bunchee out on their colas. Okay, forget it, laugh about it. At least he was gone for good.

Only not quite. Even Faustino wouldn't have laughed at that summer ahead . . . not the comic-opera cattle drive that grew directly out of his ineptitude, and mine. And most of all, not at the last seed which had been planted in his era, and now threatened to take Teddy's life.

After a five-week trip to the western Pacific, where I was researching a novel, Teddy and I, thoroughly jet-lagged, returned to Arizona, and began the ordeal of closing the house and setting out for Wyoming.

It was a madness we performed twice yearly, a last furious night spent pulling sheets over the living room furniture so it looked like a morgue. Then I'd be stuffing the Travelall with files and unwritten books, grandmother's flat silver again, plus Teddy's collection of vats and jugs for her wine making, the envy of Christian Brothers until you had to ride a thousand miles with them clinking, cats mewling amidst brown paper boxes, and Kitty Litter trays blocking any possible view out of side or rear windows. A ton of junk—dead pawn, the Indians call it; splinters of lives that no one will come and reclaim. The sheer combat loading alone would have defied the skipper of an aircraft carrier, let alone unstructural me. Why, I'd bellow at Teddy, do we have to lug up a *case* of whole-wheat crackers and two fifty-pound sacks of wheat? "Because they don't have a health-food store in Cora," Teddy would answer, surfacing from some dusty closet. "While you're at it, don't forget my flour grinder."

This metallic monster was like loading a French 75. "Someday, by God, I'm going to buy you two of everything; one for here and one for there."

"Who is it who wanted two ranches?" Teddy would point me at another monster box filled with so much soy sauce, oats, and tins of honey a wetback couldn't have budged it.

Somewhere in the night, with dogs and cats poised in the kitchen, ready for predawn take-off, I finished up my limited affairs, mainly briefing Bill Kent and a deaf old Mexican on the running of the ranch. Then, a last cooking of the feedlot books with podner, who was puffing his cheroot and saying: "Spectacular, Otis. This goddamn yearling market is out of sight!" He'd already shipped me up ten truckloads of Okie black and tans: they'd be rolling in that Wyoming grass when I got there. Six hundred head, all mine, and what they cost I didn't dare imagine.

Speaking of cattle, I said, that afternoon, to escape from Teddy's loading list, I'd fled to the feedlot for a farewell showing of the flag. Nobody seemed to be around in the corral area except sleeping black armies of cattle, and a coyote. I noticed him because I first thought he was a dog: quite a fat dog, actually, and friendly to the point of boldness. When I finally located one of our young feedlot workers, I said: "You know, that coyote came so close to me I thought he was going to pee on my leg."

"Hell, Skipper, he wouldn't do nothin' like that." The kid grinned. Good kid: ex-marine, wounded in Nam. We seemed to have most of the Old Corps here; they all called me Skipper, which was heartening. "The thing is, them coyotes got nothin' to do, except wait around in the chow line for the next dead pile."

"The what?"

He smiled and pointed his shrapneled arm at a small arroyo. As it turned out, I could have found it from the vultures alone. It was a mass grave of bones, hides, carcasses, with the feedlot workers shoveling in more from a truck. Not possibly . . . ours?

"Wal now, Otis,"—this was podner that night over the ledger books—"you gotta expect *some* death loss when you're just startin' out. Some of them Okies, you know . . . had rains back there, them cattle standing around in put-rid corrals, bound to get a little shipping fever."

We'd had very few put-rid corrals in Sonora, and certainly no rain: that is, healthy cattle. But that was *my* cattle, back then.

Podner grinned. "We got a ton of medicine pumping into 'em now, got it under control. Let it rain just a tad down here, we're gonna look spec-tacular, Otis. Best thing you can do is just go up there north and catch us a nice mess of trout."

Yeah. That probably was the best thing. So, we closed the ledger books and, as in some early war film about dawn patrols, we shook hands all around. Or was it, I wondered, an early western where the trail boss was saying: "Son, a cowboy is a feller who knows cows and don't own any. A cowman owns 'em, and don't know his ass."

And then it was morning and the cowman pointed 'em north, happy ranchers heading for the Big Pasture in the Sky.

I can't remember when the first argument with Teddy started. Probably it was just south of Phoenix where I took a back road instead of the freeway. I could drive at eighty here and get the air-conditioner up to freeze, intending to rid us of the stink one of the cats had laid. That was *my* side of the story. Teddy's was that we didn't need the thirty-dollar speeding ticket. If I hadn't been berating her, I would have seen the police car. Then the sun really came up, scorching the desert. The animals were panting, and why hadn't I taken the trouble to get the air-conditioning fixed so it would run at fifty-five? Which it would have, if *she* hadn't overloaded the car, and *she* running so late with all her last-minute flyspecking details. "You think about *that*, your hangups," I snapped, "before you have one of these packing orgies again. I'm sick of your taking every piece of string and bent pin. Do you know how you look right now, putting all this needless strain on yourself, compulsive damn cleaning and moving out as if we're never coming home again... YOU LOOK TERRIBLE!"

"Get off it!"

"Well it's true."

"I'm telling you to get off my back, dammit!"

"Isn't this brilliant conversation? Are we going to have this for two days now?"

"Just be quiet."

And happily on to Flagstaff in a grit of silence, punctuated only by essential orders to the animals surrounding us: get that damn cat off my shoulder... When we reached the city limits in the pines, Teddy saw a gas station: "Stop there." I really thought she was going to walk home... whichever way home was. Instead, she went to a pay phone and called the Tucson rug man long distance, having forgotten to tell him which rugs were to be shampooed.

"Minutiae!" I bellowed when she, quite ashen, returned to the car. "Every damn detail? Can't you let go?"

She got in beside me and curled up on the front seat. She let go all right. Tears ran down her cheeks. "I don't feel well," she murmured.

At first I was saying, See? She'd just shake her head and say, Don't. She wanted only to sleep. As the hours of afternoon sun crossed the car, she never wakened, the golden light on her face making it look strangely sallow. To have no energy or ambition, or ever to say she didn't feel well... this just wasn't Teddy. In fact, she was so wrung out, and I so humiliated by my anger, I stopped at a Navajo trading post and bought her a pair of silver earrings. Normally she's an earring addict; now she just gripped my hand, and went back to the car to sleep some more.

A night later, the soft green and cool of Wyoming, returning to this place we loved, seemed to perk her up. Working at half speed, and promising me that she'd take care of herself, she managed to get the house in order. I lined up my erasers and pipes beside my typewriter, casting only the most disciplined glance at the trout rising in the Green River. Most of all I tried to ignore the Okie cattle, which seemed to be standing unappreciatively and listlessly out in our lush pastures. I assumed it was too much of a culture shock for them. Several had already toppled over dead from no apparent cause. And our sons Peter and John, who were running the steers that summer for a share of the "profits," did confess that when the truck arrived, six other dead ones were pulled out of the dark steamy holds.

I said: Startin' out, we have to expect some death loss, okay? So put it aside. And back I went to the typewriter, to get some bread on the table. When no immediate book idea rose from the dough, I began doing travel articles about the Pacific, wishing I were back there. After my morning work was done, I'd catch Teddy's horse, saddle up, only to have her say she didn't really feel like it. Not yet. So, Pete, John, and I would ride together, eyeballing our Red River herd, until they'd spy some moldy beast, clinically describe him as "snotting at the nose." Out shot the lariats then, with rat-tat-tatting of hooves through sagebrush, badger holes, and runoff ponds left by the just melted snows. When the steer was finally hogtied, the boys would pump into him more of those wonderful medicines we were buying wholesale down at the feedlot. The steer would stagger up with a wounded look, the boys saying, "You can really pick the cattle, Big O."

After one such afternoon, I came home to find Teddy still in bed. She hadn't gotten up since breakfast. "Well, you *are* getting up now," I said, and made a call to Rock Springs, a hundred twenty miles south, where we had a friend who was a fine surgeon. Teddy was so weak I had to help dress her; she kept protesting that it was probably the flu.

When she moped into the surgeon's office, he took one look at her and said: "I'm not an internist, but I'd bet my years in medical school that she has hepatitis." He touched her face and even I could see the yellow in her eyes, the awful sallowness.

As the nurse bundled her into the car and gave her a blanket, the surgeon said: "Bad case. You get her to Salt Lake right now. I've got the best man I can find waiting for her."

The long sunset died over the Wyoming plateau and the Wasatch front. We were alone on a ribbon of interstate...a hundred fifty miles...the headlights of passing cars burning into my eyes. I kept telling her it wasn't so bad. Everybody had hepatitis sometime. As strong as she was, she'd be out riding in a couple of weeks. She just kept nodding and huddling against me under the blanket.

The past kept wrenching back. She *was* strong; she was the most vibrant, enthusiastic, life-given person I'd ever known. And yet why was it she who had to suffer? Years before, when we still lived in California, she'd had sieges of ulcers. I remembered rushing her across country on a train—she couldn't fly; her ulcers were bleeding—arriving at the Mayo Clinic in a blizzard. And waiting there through the gray days while they tested her. A young doctor finally sat us down in his office and said: "Look, young lady. There is absolutely no reason for you to have ulcers this badly."

"But, if you operate," Teddy asked hesitantly, "won't they go away?"

"I'll never operate on you. Because you're going to take them away yourself. Yes. Turn it off in your head, because that's where they begin. Stop trying to be all things to all people, hurling yourself into everything. You're not indispensable!"

Slowly, Teddy did manage to turn it off, and the ulcers went away. Never totally, always an occasional flare-up when she'd fall back. I tried to be optimistic that night in the car. Hepatitis was something that came from the outside. It wasn't part of her. This was just a bug, to beat.

The doctor hospitalized her on arrival. Total rest was the only cure, and of course, staying off the booze. Teddy could smile at this. She rarely drank anything except her home-brew wine. Not even that, the doctor said. A week later, when we left the hospital and drove back to the ranch, I was sure she was on the road to recovery. One of the top liver specialists in the area had been called in on her case. Though I hadn't personally heard this doctor's opinion, apparently he was equally hopeful.

As to why hepatitis would suddenly strike her, one doctor said, "Well, it could have come from anyplace. But the fact that you've just returned from several islands in the Pacific, where I understand it's abysmally dirty . . . she might well have contracted it there."

So much for second honeymoons.

In fact, the night I brought Teddy home from the hospital, I was just pulling down the blinds when our bedroom began to glow with silver. The moon was burning through the dark fingers of lodgepole pines on Black Butte, then racing pale across the hay meadows until it lay in the oxbow of the Green River beneath us, etching the powerful water into changeable flutings that could have been the side of a punchbowl, or an engraved tray to serve champagne on.

The spring of the Okies was definitely behind us. The reason we knew—this night of June 21 was the first day of summer. And, for better or worse, our twenty-sixth wedding anniversary.

2

Summer of the Elk

One morning in early July, I was riding through our Okie
steers. In a pasture just above the Green River, they dotted
the soft hills of sagebrush like lumps of coal. As I
approached them, a few of the wary ones began pushing
up lazily and stretching. That's when I noticed something
red in their midst. Possibly a stray, I thought, because it
didn't move. Actually, it was a dull rusty-colored animal
with a long neck and a head that didn't fit a bovine. I
edged my horse closer, then stopped short. Munching cud
in the grass was an elk.

I was delighted, astounded. Elk are the wildest of our
game animals, and certainly the spookiest. At this time of

summer they should have been hiding ten thousand feet up in the remote black timber. Yet here this one lay, within a mile of our ranch house, pretending for all the world to be a steer.

At the sight of me, the elk gave a little sniff, then sprang up leggily and trotted off a few yards. She was a young cow, maybe two or three years old, and dry, that is, without calf. I circled her several times. She made no effort to run away. When I turned and galloped back toward the ranch house, I reined in once and stared at her from a distance, as if to make certain she wasn't an apparition. But there she was, cricking down until she lay again in the grass, surrounded by her coal-black friends.

Right after lunch, I insisted on bringing Teddy and our foreman, John Fandek, out to see her. John is a well-known nature photographer, and this was certainly a time for his camera, or else nobody would believe us. In his patient way, he dismounted and managed to wriggle his way to within a few feet of her. She never even stood up, merely cocked her graceful neck as if she were a society model, posing in the wildflowers for *Town and Country*.

At this point we were certain that she had to be sick, or at the very least was packing around a bullet from last fall's hunt. But since John had often fed elk for the state of Wyoming during the winters, driving a team and hay sled out to them daily, he had an excellent eye for their condition. Definitely, he said, there wasn't a mark on her, and the sheen of her coat and moistness of nose belied any illness.

A few days later when we moved the steers to the higher pastures, she bounded along with the herd leaders, just as agile and fit as any elk in the wild. When the steers would shade up and fight flies in the fringes of aspen, she'd burrow in next to them, the closer the better, it seemed, as if she wanted to put on one of their black Okie hides.

Soon, her presence became an event in the neighborhood, which doesn't have many, considering that our town of Cora boasts a population of three. That's downtown Cora. There are more people out on the ranches, of course, and now many of these grizzled cowboys were shaking their heads and saying: "Reckon we'd better go see that there tame elk Carneys has got." So up would rattle the pickup trucks, or we'd have fishing friends at the ranch and we'd swing through the aspen groves for a look at her. "Why don't you name her?" somebody suggested, but frankly I regarded the arrangement as too impermanent for that. We'd ride out some morning and she'd be gone. That's what had happened to Agnes, our pet antelope, and Gladys, the world's ugliest moose, which hung around our house so fearlessly she used to delight in breathing on our windows, and then rubbing the mist off with her nose. It was hard to see such companions leave, and depressing to think of them ending up quartered in some hunter's freezer. So it was better just to remain at arm's length and let nature take its course.

Yet strangely, that summer, I found myself often slipping into the timber alone, hunkering down on a log, and watching the cow elk. It was obvious what she had done: she was simply imprinting on another specie. And she was damn good at it, this female impersonator trying to be what she wasn't.

Trying to live someone else's life. And wasn't that, I had to ask, exactly my problem? Trying to be what I was not. The ranches, the feedlot. Certainly I hadn't been born to this lifestyle. Maybe somewhere in my grandfather's County Mayo, Ireland, a Carney had been a drover of beasts, but such a lad was far back in the lineage, as far as I could tell. As for the writing side of me, not one author I knew, in control of his senses, would allow himself to be bogged down with the two-headed ranch company I was trying to run. No, if you wrote, you wrote. Oh, perhaps if you were Ernest Gann, you could permit yourself a small, uncomplicated stunt airplane, so you could go out and snap roll your brains back into place when the typewriter had pounded them into gibberish. Yet, beyond such momentary diversion, you really had to *center* on what you did. I, however, like the elk, was trying to be two creatures at once.

One part of me was the structured, rational "western man," trained for competition, for conquest and material rewards. This inner man was always looking restlessly into the future, for new skies to tame. He was in a process of *becoming*.

Yet the other part of me was already *there*. He was the free spirit, the primitive, perfectly content with the present, with *being*, because in this rootedness, he found himself linked to a comforting rhythm that was the soulbeat of all mankind, past and future. In the unfolding of his uniqueness, he thus felt an innate nobility: that he *counted* in God's plan, just because he was living out his tiny but essential part of it.

For this reason, he would never know the dismay of "quiet desperation," the plodding lockstep of a life without meaning. Instead, his connection to God gave him his sense of completeness.

This struggle between the two parts of me was a symptom of our age—a dilemma neatly framed by writer Peter Steinhardt in comments to the Audubon Society. "Only repeatable fact," he said, "is held to be the source of truth in modern culture. Science is unable to admit of love or the will to live. Churches direct us to obedient readings of the scripture rather than receptivity to new voices. There are messages for which our culture cannot find a proper voice. Consequently, our age is filled with supernatural longings and angry cynicism. One may embrace flying saucers but deny the existence of Allah, trust the president one day and laugh at him the next. We seek guidance, *but we aren't sure who the guide is.*

"That is why," continued Steinhardt, "we talk to the animals. They see and hear what we see and hear, but they have none of our crippling doubts."

The elk and I. Doubts indeed! Who, really, were we? Which creature within us would be the guide?

And, more maddening to me in my search was still another statement that I'd clipped and taped above my typewriter. This was a prediction, a glimpse at a future when the war in me and so many others might finally be surrendered. In his classic speech at Harvard, novelist Alexander Solzhenitsyn had said:

"The turn toward inward development will be a great turning point in the history of mankind, comparable to the transition from the Middle Ages to the Renaissance. There will be a complete change in the very nature of human beings, a change from spiritual dispersal to spiritual concentration. This ascension will be similar to climbing onto the next anthropologic stage. No one on earth has any way left but upward."

Was this, I wondered, where I and so many others were heading in our struggle to develop the inner man? And how incredibly powerful the prediction was, coming from Solzhenitsyn who had suffered the ultimate failure of a materialist-humanist culture. When man discovered that he could not live by bread alone, he had no choice but to turn inward, to reconnect to his long abandoned and darkly shadowed spiritual self. This yearning was his center, and always had been. Now, instead of dispersing his spirit into the worldly worships of technology, political power, wealth, hedonism—or of making a god of himself—man would learn to concentrate his spirit upward, toward God where it belonged. In this ultimate battle, he would bring a change in himself that would change the world.

It was that exact longing, I realized, that had brought me back to the land, to a quiet, hard-rock arena where such difficult change might be forged.

So which was the true elk? Which part of me was in command? I had to find out now. I thirsted for the answer, so that I could begin to live it!

And, of course, like all those who seek transcendence, I wanted it yesterday. Wanted to *be there*, take the twelve easy lessons, get my diploma and have peace!

But life has a wonderfully insulating slowness on a ranch, as if Nature knows man's awful impatience, and simply refuses to yield up her secrets all at once. Yet with a goal seen now, I found myself at least listening for clues from my environment.

On a July morning I guided one of my oldest friends on a search for brook trout. I brought him to a particular pond in a valley of aspen because it was the best water we had for trophy fish. He was that kind of man, my friend; he always went for the big ones, and I admired him greatly. As we crept up on the log dam, I noted a purpling, sultry silence in an old dark channel that ran between two swatches of weeds. "Drop a nymph in there," I whispered, "very slowly. Make one cast and make it perfect."

His line looped out. The fly dapped in, exactly as I'd told him. Nothing happened. When he finally retrieved his fly, it was covered with mucky moss. "Well," he said, "I'll clean it off and shoot it again."

But as he stood on the dam, with the cottony clouds racing above us and darkening the sun, his face tightened and his fingers no longer plucked at the fly. Finally he murmured, "I don't know about your life. But I can tell you this for sure: mine is a goddamn mess."

"Aw, come on."

"No, I mean it."

"In what way?"

"Just that... where's it all going? What's it been for? Ah, hell." He shrugged and began to concentrate on his fishing.

Maybe it was the shadow now, or the barometric

pressure, but the fish began to work. Within a few minutes, he'd caught three heavy, deep-bellied brook trout. They were slashing, noble fighters. When the last trout ensnared himself in a mass of weeds, my friend plunged into the icy water and seized the fish in his bare hands. Yet later, when he held up his trophies so I could photograph them, there was still a sadness in his smile.

If I wanted a role model in my life, this man would be it. He'd racked up all the gold stars: he'd been an athlete, a wartime pilot, fathered a large and outstanding family and remained a good friend to even the humblest people who'd crossed his path. In his vision and courage, he'd become a leader in his profession, climbing from success to success until I couldn't think of one thing he lacked. Love, wealth, fame: he had them all, yet apparently without satisfaction or peace.

He was still hurrying on restlessly, leaving the ranch that afternoon, to seek some other new action in a business meeting, some acquisition, after which there'd be another rushing trip to sample another of his many lifestyles, in his world filled with so many good and admiring friends.

As I watched his dust curl up the road toward Black Butte, I could only think, there but for the grace of God go I. We'd ridden the same commuting trains together in the old days. And now, did I want to go back with him again to more of the same? To reach what? To reach the top, and have his sadness in my smile?

I shuddered, thinking about it.

Now that Teddy was back in our sun-filled bedroom overlooking the Green, I resolved to coddle her like an egg until she was completely recovered. I gave her strict orders that she was not to lift a finger, but simply leave the entire household to me. At the time, domestic chores seemed a helluva lot easier than finding a new book to write.

Well, it was a nice try, against impossible odds. To get Teddy to give up her house was like unplugging her cat, Electra, from her three kittens. I burned my way through all our saucepans, preparing her proper bland diet: daily boilovers, spills, shatters of glass. My last serious cooking had been done under the wing of our plane at Pelelieu, using a cartridge-case liner as a stove. The crew didn't like it, but I was the only mess around. Now, however, John, Pete, and their legions of drop-in friends simply burrowed into the bunkhouse at mealtime, preferring to batch their own. It was galling to me that my sons were such competent cooks, their generation apparently not reject-ing the apron image as I had. After a week or so, I raided the local stores, wiping out their larder of TV dinners: Teddy despises the things. Finally she sat up limply in bed and announced, "This just isn't going to work."

The problem was, we'd been invaded by the locusts of summer. I've never understood how so many people have so little to do in July and August, and invariably manage to show up in our remote corner of Wyoming. You can't even find Cora with a magnifying glass: it's the farthest point from a railroad in the U.S., and our airports, though closer, are still long pounding hours through the moun-tains. Yet in came humping Volkswagen buses, back-packers, hitchhikers, and then, old so-and-so from some distant corner of our lives—wheeling up, stationwagon gleaming with fishing rods and bright orange tents for the wife and kiddies. We had every valid reason to send packing these "dry dudes," as the locals call nonpayers, but by the time they had lurched up our long dusty road, we simply didn't have the heart to turn them away. Then they'd get so exhausted riding our horses and catching our fish that they couldn't possibly leave. A one-night stay would expand into three. If they had any strong-backed teenagers in their group, John and Pete would eagerly seize them for the wetback chores they didn't want to do themselves. In addition, there were friends of the boys and friends of friends, whose only connection with our family often seemed to be that we were all Americans. At night the bunkhouse would echo with rock-beating amplified guitars and the wailing of now-generation balladeers.

Help! we pleaded, and ironically it came from the young. Let any busty hippie girl hike up our trail, we'd remove her mandolin and brazenly beg her to be our "summer girl." These wandering ladies seemed always to be en route to "meaningful experience": lovers to live with and peaks to climb, and the antithesis of liberation was to be chained to a kitchen under the grubby title of household domestic. They all wanted to "work with animals" or collect ferns. We hired on a welder's daughter who was brighter than most college professors; she'd mastered German philosophy but her attempts at cooking convinced me that she must have been fed intravenously all her life. When I tried to show another girl how to blend up the health-vegetable soups Teddy loves, that young lady managed to screw on the blender in such a way that the fan blades ate it. We had ground-glass broth. When she left, in drifted an angry activist, just off the barricades at Berkeley. It wasn't hamburgers for dinner, but an hour's diatribe as to why we were still in Vietnam. As migrant after migrant drifted away in sandals, I got desperate and began calling old ladies...hay cooks, hunting cooks, grandmothers in Mexico. Nobody. It was me and the high oven, all alone. "Oh, get with it, Big O," the boys would say. "It's just the *idea* of cooking that offends you, you're such an elitist." Then they'd pile into the ranch truck with guitars, and head off for a big blowout in town.

In the old days, when the boys had been bucking hay bales, their summer game had been touch football, to get them into shape for more serious gridiron battles back at school or college come autumn. Now, however, focus had shifted to rodeo, and not a gentleman's event like calf roping but, instead, the teeth-jamming macho of riding bareback broncs. As I'd patiently point out: suppose they broke a leg or worse? Who then, except Teddy and I, would handle the care and feeding of six hundred Okie steers? They never gave it a thought. On rodeo nights each week, I'd lie beside Teddy in bed, waiting for the thrum of the tires on the cattle guard, signaling that our riders had made it home in one piece. On several mornings-after, a few survivors didn't get up, and occasionally I'd catch John or Pete, hobbling around with sheepish grins. One night when there was a really big rodeo, they asked me to come in and see firsthand what harmless fun it was.

I sat up in that dark grandstand, clinging to a beer and wishing I were in a foxhole when the first bronc came careening out. I thought John was on him. But no, just a tough nut of a cowboy kid. The bronc, deciding not to buck but to run, came thundering at the grandstand and flung the kid over the six-foot fence, almost into my lap.

Pete was next. But the chute gate never opened. I saw a scuffle, a glint of the horse's forefeet up and pawing as he toppled over backward and began tromping Pete into the chute boards. Pete came out spitting blood, cursing: lousy damn horse, and they'd better give him another ride. They did, and he got bucked off after the first few jumps.

Next rider, crackled the loudspeaker: "John Carney on Grandmother Killer" or some aptly named cayuse. John was a blur of jerks and lunges, his arm fanning wildly under the arena lights. He stayed on the bronc, the audience giving appreciative horn beeps as he rode it out to the buzzer. The pickup man was just galloping in to snatch him to safety when, with one last flip, the bronc cartwheeled and John was lying face down in the dirt. A full minute later he shook himself and got up. I'd watched him play football for years; he'd take a hit, shake it off, and walk away. This time, instead of going out of the arena, he seemed not to know where out was. He wandered to the fence by the grandstand and sat down, his head curling into his knees. I didn't want to show too much concern: cowboy parents don't *do* that, so I just idled along the fence and whispered: "John?"

When his face drifted up, it was as green-yellow as Teddy's with hepatitis. "Let's go," he said.

"Where'd it get you?"

His fingers touched his shoulder. "Here."

A nice thing about rodeo is that our local doctor wouldn't miss one for the world. He was waiting at the fence to scrape John up. It was a beautiful clean little break, he said ... just a collarbone. John vomited from the pain while the doctor was setting it; then, he simply brushed the manure off his Levi's and took me with him to the local cowboy bar where such events were always celebrated. Even with his bandaged shoulder, John played guitar along with Pete and the others. People began to dance and I finally joined them, figuring I'd gotten off easy. I could just as well have been biting my fingernails in intensive care.

I drifted up to a rosy-cheeked girl I'd seen before with the boys. She had Godiva-like blonde tresses that spilled down her shoulders. I was puzzled as to whether in the etiquette of the youth group, one put his hand *over* or *under* this waterfall of spun gold. I also didn't catch her name, until her blue eyes sparkled up at mine. "It's Rita."

"Irish?"

"What do you think?"

I thought she was pretty cute, frankly, and said that to Pete when I sat down beside him. He nodded: "Glad you like her. She's going to be our new cook."

"What? Who said ... ?"

"I said."

A few days later, Rita moved in with us. She'd been working at a nearby guest ranch, until Pete convinced her that ours was a better job. "Reet's from a big family," Pete shrugged casually. "She can handle all the people we've got around here." One thing she could clearly handle was the kitchen stove. Suddenly the meals appeared beautifully served on trays, without political diatribe. The fact that Pete hung around Rita in the kitchen and while she was making the beds didn't seem to bother Teddy. "I think Rita can handle him better than we can," she'd say. Indeed, there was a fire in Rita that managed miraculously to get Pete up at first dawn: they'd be saddling horses or plunging into the icy Green. We were convinced it was some other kid out there, not laid-back Pete. Whatever it was, I thought, don't knock it. I was finally freed from the stove, Teddy clearing resting and improving. Though I hadn't sold any of the Pacific articles (they were not "travel-conducive," the editors said), I was still hoping that lightning would strike with a new idea for a novel. Exactly then, an old friend invited me to go fishing with him in British Columbia.

Teddy insisted that I go. It was my turn for a rest now. I packed my flyrod and fled, hoping that some rushing river in B.C. would loose a torrent of words from me.

When I came home three days later, Peter and John met me before I entered the house. "We want you to get it from us," they warned, "and don't listen to Fred (their name for Teddy, Frederika). Most of all, don't get freaked at what she did. It was...well, sort of a misunderstanding."

A spec-tacular misunderstanding, as it turned out. The afternoon I left, Pete and John had been riding through the steers in the upper pastures. Hidden among the aspen, they found two dead ones, sprawled and bloating, and to their horror, saw dozens of others with a telltale swelling in their chests. The verdict, confirmed quickly by the vet and neighbors, was big brisket. If a steer has had pulmonary sickness in the spring...if he comes from a low altitude (the damn Georgia swamps and pu-trid corrals)... and is moved into our 8,600-foot mountains, his pleural cavity simply swells up with fluid. He's almost certain to die unless you immediately rush him back down to where he can breathe.

On the night of that happy diagnosis, a council of war was held at the ranch house. According to the boys, Teddy was Scarlett O'Hara, fighting the Yankees at the gates: she was up out of bed, arranging for cattle trucks to haul the steers to Salt Lake, our closest low altitude: hurrying, worrying, calling neighbors. They, God bless them, responded in a rush the next morning, even tacking up Teddy's horse because she was so weak and yellow she didn't look as if she could lift her small English saddle. The neighbors pleaded with her to stay in bed, but she'd have none of it. She went out and rode for hours in the sagebrush, helping sort the bulging chests from the merely normal snotnoses.

Then, according to the boys, late that afternoon everything started going wrong, and they and Teddy learned a lesson from a remarkable old cowboy named Rex.

He was a prototype of the vanishing breed. With his Roman nose and handlebar moustache, he surely didn't look his eighty years, probably because most of them had been spent atop a horse. As the chief rider for the Green River Valley Cattlemens Association, Rex had eleven thousand of his own cows and calves to beat down out of the mountains before the snow. Then too, one time when Rex had helped us in the past, I sent him twenty-five dollars. In the return mail I received a note: "I will drink your whisky and be your friend. But I will not except mony for layin my roap on some dam cow." Inside his grubby piece of copybook paper was my neatly folded check.

This time, Rex was the key neighbor who'd come to help Teddy with the roundup. The other assistants, beside

John and Pete, were two twelve-year-old girls, excellent riders, but with over five hundred cranky beasts to move, they needed all the help they could get.

What had gone wrong was the weather. Fairly typical of later summer in Wyoming, a violent mountain storm had swirled up in the dusk. As the clouds lowered and tore apart in angry lashes of rain, down through the sagebrush came Rex and the herd of sodden steers. At first he was hard to distinguish, because he was far in the rear, patiently brushing the stragglers toward the bunch. By now, the boys said, Teddy's felt hat was drooping over her ears and her slicker shining black. In her chilled exhaustion, there was a frantic sort of hurry about her, the way she'd spur in at the herd and keep the pressure on the would-be escapers. That's the moving of dumb beasts, of course. They always know how to beat you. And in the wet and the mud, you can turn your horse too quick. He'll slip out from under you or step in a badger hole that he hasn't seen.

At that moment, however, everyone had seen where the wreck was going to take place: our plank bridge across the Green River. In the freezing rain, the first steers had just touched their hooves and noses on the narrow bridge. They hesitated, smelling the strange wetness. When the hundreds of other steers came milling and bleating in behind them, it was like a panic in an elevator. The lead steers whirled and bolted from the bridge, ripping back through the entire herd, which began leaping and running, squirting off in all directions, some of them crashing down through the willows and falling into the river. Others were thundering across the sagebrush, Teddy, John, Pete, and the twelve-year-old girls whipping their horses to get ahead, turn them.

Pandemonium. And where was Rex? He was simply huddled off to one side, watching, with his forearm resting on his saddle horn.

Presently he did turn his horse and began to walk slowly back through the sagebrush. It seemed to take him hours to reach the last divider fence, as if he knew the steers couldn't get through this. He was right. They'd raced up to the wires and bundled into a swirling stop. Slowly, then, Rex moved along the fence and started them again toward the hated bridge.

When they reached it the second time, they reacted exactly the same way: more panic, bawling, splashing into the river ... and pell-mell back to the divider fence.

Three times more they did this; Rex never took his horse out of a walk, and always managed to retrieve the herd. On the fourth try—now it was almost dark—the steers crowded sullenly against the funnel of barbed wire that led onto the bridge. Rex edged in next to Teddy, and because her horse was lathered and restless, Rex patted the colt's shoulder and pushed him gently aside.

At that moment, a steer took the first step onto the bridge. He sniffed it, and froze. But now, as he looked around, a second, then a third steer moved in beside him. They stared at each other, but not for long, because behind them they seemed to sense a slow, quiet presence. They turned their heads. Rex had somehow slipped through the herd, but now neither he nor his horse moved a muscle. Rex didn't really block the entrance to the bridge. He was simply there, holding the first three steers so they couldn't turn back. Rex's silence seemed impenetrable. The steers thought about it, and then slowly took another step or two forward on the bridge. Almost imperceptibly, Rex's "presence" eased to one side, allowing more steers to follow the first. By now the leaders were halfway across the bridge. Then, one of them kicked and bucked, and leaped out toward the far side, a glorious thunder of hooves tocking hollowly on wood. The entire heard was sweeping into the funnel and racing across the bridge, moving on the dead run straight down the muddy road to the corrals.

When the riders finally came back to the house, they all, except Teddy, had joyous "whisky," in thanks to Rex for laying his "roap on our dam cows." When the boys had asked him how he did it, he stroked the wetness out of his handlebar mustache and grinned. "Jest...slow," he said. "Slowin' 'em...."

As he'd told Teddy at the last critical moment on the bridge: "Little lady, God made twenty-four hours in each day. I reckon we's entitled to enjoy every minute of every one of 'em."

But unfortunately, when I'd returned the following night. I was unable to appreciate the wisdom of Rex's patience, let alone live it. Teddy seemed to have aged years in the days I'd been gone. Her eyes were dark, her skin ashen. The helpless way she lay in bed made me hug her; she felt hot beneath my fingers, her bones aching at any motion. "Now why did you do that?" I whispered.

"I'm fine, really. Just tired."

I tried to tell her I never would have gone had I known such a thing would happen. She touched my lips and shushed me weakly; then she lay down again and simply slept.

The next morning I called her doctor in Salt Lake. He was off on a fishing trip himself. Then we called another old friend, an internist in California, who was understandably reluctant to diagnose over the telephone. All we really learned was that hepatitis could be awfully hard to lick. Teddy should just rest some more and stop worrying about cattle.

That was my job, and meanwhile out in the sagebrush, the Okies were dropping fast. We'd lost nearly eleven percent of them so far, when the normal rate should have been under three percent. Then, late one night, my podner called from Arizona. He sounded as if he were telephoning from Diablo Canyon, which was as far away as he could get. Things, he reported, were something short of spec-tacular.

I steeled myself. "Cattle dying?"

"Wal, a fella always expects some of that. But mostly, it ain't rainin'. Not a tad of rain. You couldn't part your hair with what we got this summer . . ." By now I was wincing with him as he marched me through the various pastures where nothing remained but burroweed.

"Okay, what are we going to do?"

His voice trailed back. "No choice. We've got to sell early, unless you want what's left of this ranch to burn up and blow away." Then he began a mournful litany of numbers, how he'd figured it, and the accountants had figured, and by selling early we were going to lose X-thousand pounds of beef times the contracted sale price. On the other hand, getting out early might prove the smartest thing in the world, if Nixon was going to freeze us . . .

"Nixon what?"

"Wal, that's the rumor. Because of speculatin' and runnin' beef up so high, Nixon's gonna freeze the fat market. That'll make steers plumb worthless in a couple of weeks . . . aw, maybe not totally, just that the fellers buyin' 'em are gonna lose a minimum of a hundred dollars a head."

All this and Nixon too. It didn't seem possible.

"Course," my partner added generously, "he's playin' good politics. This is gonna mean lower beef prices for the consumer, and there's a hal-acious more of consumers than there is of us . . ."

Very few of us, in fact . . . with our Okie herd marching suicidally off into the sunset. But then my podner tried to cheer me up, the way Faustino used to. "I'm looking up at clouds right now that is trying to rain. And we're damn lucky that my contact who's buyin' these steers is ready to eat 'em this early. He could have just walked away, downpayment or no, and leave us stuck with the whole bunch."

The last bunchee, out on their colas. Well, by then I didn't care about briskets or books or anything except Teddy. She lay in bed, hollow-eyed and drawn, so listless she could barely speak. Though Rita was still running the house beautifully, there was just too much of it, too many friends, and a telephone that wouldn't stop ringing. I made up my mind I was going to pluck Teddy out of here, take her to a good hotel someplace and let room service cure her. The problem...where? Anything in the Cora Valley would be a motel or dude ranch, and why buy when we were running one ourselves? I got into the car and raced over to Jackson. Maybe something in the Rockefeller lodges? They were sold out, with waiting lists. The afternoon I returned, Teddy's headache was so bad she couldn't sit up for more than a minute or so. I practically carried her to the car, as I'd done that first night going to Rock Springs. This time, we'd go direct to Salt Lake, the pillared splendor of the Hotel Utah where, by morning, I'd get a doctor to see her.

It was midnight before we trooped upstairs in the hotel to a large rococo suite, customarily given over to lingerie salesmen with their display cases. The furniture had claws for feet and looked like a lion pack crouching in jungle shadows. The bed was as big as the African Queen. I lolled Teddy into it, and now we were certain that in such opulent isolation, everything would look better in the morning.

The doctor, it turned out, had to leave town on some other emergency, coincident with Labor Day weekend. No, he didn't have an assistant, and when Teddy couldn't even eat breakfast, I knew I had to find somebody, fast. Yet where? We were strangers in Salt Lake, living so far away...and we were certainly strangers to any kind of doctor, for we never seemed to be sick. Finally it snapped into my mind: the young consultant on Teddy's case. Could she remember his name?

It had been two months before; she couldn't. I got out the telephone book and we filmed over the names... sounded like, rhymes with...*zow*, she got it. Anglo-Saxon Mormon name, and the angel Moroni must have been up there beaming on us, because this young ex-airforce internist happened not to be treating big brisket or out on the ninth tee. He was dutifully sitting in his office as if he knew we'd call.

I rushed Teddy up there and she disappeared with him into the examining room. She never came out. Instead, he took her the back way directly to the same hospital where she'd been in June. The Holy Cross and its white-robed nuns. But this time, they wouldn't let me into her room, and the nurses who entered wore face masks and surgical gowns. Up went the red sign: Contagious.

What? Hepatitis?

The internist countered with scientific jargon about something called "the Australian antogen." When I didn't understand, he said: "She has hepatitis in her bloodstream. That's different from ordinary hepatitis. Rarer, more dangerous. The real problem is, it's quite far advanced. From her liver biopsy, it's clear that it has gone into chronic aggressive liver disease, and I can assume that she's lost about twenty-five percent of her liver right now. That happens with some people. It just eats their liver up. Destroys it."

He said so much, so fast, I couldn't get it, and didn't want to believe. I kept mumbling: well, how could this have happened? Maybe the dirt of the Pacific, something picked up out there...?

"Not this," the internist said. "We see it in...well, drug addicts, who take a lot of injections. Dirty needles. She doesn't do that, of course. The only injection she can remember...apparently you'd had a Mexican foreman, and Mrs. Carney had gone with his wife down to Mexico for a flu shot, gamma globulin?"

I almost groaned it. "Faustino's wife!"

"Whatever," he said. "That gamma globulin in Mexico is not screened like ours. You're apt to get a hepatic donor. We'll never prove it, but the time of the incubation is exactly right, to have been caused by that flu shot." Then he handed me a pamphlet prepared by the Mayo Clinic. "This explains the disease; read it, so you'll know what she's up against. Come back first thing in the morning..."

"Yes, but..." I began, "when your liver is destroyed..."

He'd already gone back down the hall, the door to Teddy's room closing silently behind him.

In my journalism days, I used to write enough medical articles to have a passing acquaintance with scientific language and statistical charts. But when the case histories leapt up at me from the Mayo Clinic pamphlet, these weren't numbers, remote ciphers. They were Teddy. I flicked the pages angrily, racing to the end, the final chart. At the time of the Mayo Study, the mortality rate for chronic aggressive liver disease was upwards of ninety percent!

I flung the pamphlet to the floor, and lay down on the big African Queen bed. In the shadows of the ghastly rococo room, I could hear her; feel her warmth beside me. I closed my eyes, as if to hold it. And the black bars of numbers and doctor voices slammed down on me like an iron grid! No more, they said. So impersonal: she is ninety percent gone. The room began to swim before my eyes: not tears. Rage! And I saw again the times that Teddy and I had fought...those unnecessary quarrels shared by all husbands and wives. You want to hurt the other, get in one last dig. And yet every time I'd start, I knew that in hurting her, I might just as well have been slicing my own arm with a knife. Mine was hers. We were one.

How did I put that into words, when all I could hear were those grim voices of terror: diagnosing, fumbling, failing, taking her! And the needlessness of it, the idiocy. I might as well have been driving drunk, smashing her into a wall. I did this! My restless ill-content, my second ranch she didn't want, overtaxing her, dragging her half way around the world to some romantic, infantile dream. So needless, when all I could have done was simply treasure her, protect her. I stared at the bed the maid had turned down for us. Teddy's nightgown was folded on the pillow, and the tiny black glint on the night-table was her rosary.

Distant, down the hall, I could hear the whispers of television; then, the heat of the dark city, sucking in through the big opened window. The curtains riffled, and far off, a siren passed. Sometime much later, in my fear, I knelt there beside the bed with my face in my hands, until the city was long gone. The world had died for this moment, and in its silence, its not-mattering, I seemed to be stripped, emptied: humbled, until I could no longer distinguish my voice, its curses and pleas. Something else was there, some distant memory that said: Have no fear. I am with you.

When I went to the hospital the next morning, I cracked the door to Teddy's room and heard voices whispering. Then a nurse shooed me away. I paced the hall and wanted to kick down the door. Finally I found another nurse who reluctantly suited me up in hospital gown, face mask, and rubber gloves. Several grim-faced doctors filed out, mumbling in their masks. By then, although no one had given permission, I simply barged in.

Sunlight. A large-framed woman was jerking open the blinds, and turned to me with a red Irish face in her nun's halo. "Mister Carney!" she exclaimed. "What have you done to Tom, John, and Peter's lovely mother!" Then she enveloped me in a hug of white robes, like some enormous St. Bridget. I didn't have the foggiest notion who she was.

"Can you believe it, Ote?" Teddy cried. "Sister Charles Margaret. She taught the boys second grade at Beverly Hills Catholic!"

What I couldn't believe was the laughter in Teddy's eyes; in all of ours, then. Teddy was sitting up in bed, and Sister Charles Margaret was plumping her pillows and putting a big breakfast in front of her. Something had happened indeed, because the next thing demanded was Teddy's lace-fringed bedjacket and pearls to put on her neck. She ate, and we talked and laughed about old times and how far everybody had come from Beverly Hills. When Sister finally swept out in her white robes, leaving us alone, I gripped Teddy.

"What the hell is happening?"

"Some kind of miracle," she whispered. "It's a drug, very new, almost experimental. And we've got to pray I can take it. Not everybody can. It's terrible for ulcers." She rattled a bottle of pills at me.

Prednizone was the name, a powerful cortisone derivative, which, in some process I couldn't possibly understand, was the only thing that appeared to stop the deterioration caused by chronic aggressive liver disease. In the Mayo Clinic study I'd read the night before, the mortality rate had been ninety percent. Now, the new drug was the hope to cure the disease.

"But you've got to be ready for this," Teddy added. "It's so strong, if it doesn't tear up my stomach, it does grisly things like putting hair on my face, a hump on my back, and I can swell up to a hundred fifty pounds."

The only way to answer that was to hold her hundred twenty pounds, hug her, which I'd been waiting for all the night before.

"I've taken it twice already," she said. "There's been

no side effect yet. I just can't believe how well I feel. Do you think I'm imagining it? Is it really going to work?"

I held her to me, and both of us seemed to know it was. We knew nothing about medicine, but something here had turned around, in her voice and will; her faith.

Three days later, she was incredibly improved. They even let her walk up and down the hospital corridor. But only for a few minutes each day. "No hump, no hairs," I crowed to the doctor. "Look at her!"

"And for the rest of her life she'll never be able to get tired again," the doctor answered, waggling a finger at both of us. "She's a long way from any cattle drives. Those, and her mountain climbing, are a thing of the past."

"We'll see," Teddy said. But even then, she barely had strength to climb back into bed.

A few weeks later, I made a last trip to Wyoming to close the ranch house for winter. I'd left Teddy behind in an apartment we'd rented in Salt Lake. It was only a few blocks from the hospital, where she went daily for a blood analysis. Rita was still taking care of her, and both of them insisted I clear out and shoot some ducks. It might improve my disposition, which was not exactly bursting with optimism right then. Despite the drug, Teddy's recovery was haltingly slow, and when I wasn't nursing her, I'd be pecking grimly at my calculator, trying to figure out how much the feedlot was going to lose us, and how I could ever have been so stupid to get involved in it.

Wyoming had frozen by the time I arrived. Under a dark snowy sky, mist rose from the Green River and the duck ponds in the meadows were slabs of gray ice. Everyone had gone south, and I was going to have to go too, dreading it. Our banker in Arizona had said on the telephone: "Otis, when you get this feedlot all boiled

down, how much are you going to be able to wring out of
the assets?'' I gave him an estimate that Podner had
supplied, a massive fire-saling of all rolling stock, down
even to piles of steer manure that summer gardeners could
use. I could hear the banker's calculator totting away.
"All right," he continued, "when I whack fifteen percent
off what you *think* you'll get for the junk, I come up with
$90,000 you're going to owe me; $45,000 each. How's that
sound?''

How it sounded was as bleak as the wind whistling
down the Green River. As I looked across at the log
corrals, I found myself remembering my last glimpse of
those cursed Okie steers. It had been several weeks earlier,
judgment day, when we gathered the survivors, weighed
them, and hotshotted them into the trucks that would take
them to their hapless buyer. The market crash had even
upped the ante for this poor devil. Now, instead of a
hundred dollars a head, he'd probably lose two hundred.
But at least he represented a big corporate farming
operation, and I was comforted to believe that they
wouldn't hurt as much as we had.

But that morning there'd been a more poignant drama
than the steers. When we'd rattled them across the bridge
and into the corrals, along with them came their loyal
friend, the dry cow elk. I'd spotted her from horseback.
She was trotting in the lead of the herd, her head high in
the air. She began sniffing the diesel fumes of the trucks,
and was obviously confused at the bawling and the
chowsing cries of horsemen. But when the steers swept
into the corrals, she didn't try to escape. "Now what in the
hell do we do?'' asked a neighboring cowboy. "How do we
get rid of her?''

At first we tried to cut her back, as you do with a steer,
but she wasn't cutting. She'd bolt and break and beat us.
She belonged with those steers, that's what she was telling
us—indeed, she seemed to be shouting it out to me. So we

narrowed them into the tighter corrals and began sorting them for the scale. Stifflegged, she bolted past the men with whips. "Why, damn you ugly thing!" cried a cowboy. "Are you figgerin' to get on there and be weighed by the pound?"

Only by blocking her with two horses could we keep her off the scales. To divert her from what was happening, somebody tossed hay out for her. She wouldn't touch it. Her eyes kept flicking over the steers as they were hotshotted up the chute and into the trembling tin of the big trucks. When they were all loaded and gone like a cortege of hearses drumming off under leaden skies, she stood alone in the corral, then snorted and began to bolt from one end to the other. We couldn't let her out for fear she'd run up the road after them and hook her leg in a cattleguard someplace.

Finally, when the scent of them had blown away, I did open the gate. She wandered out, her head snapping from side to side, sniffing, searching. Sometime that night she crossed the bridge and walked the fences of the lower pastures, the familiar trails she'd traveled in her sojourn into another world. For several days she hung around. I'd try to get close to her, but now her black eyes would bead at me in fear and distrust. As she snorted and trotted away, I felt like calling after her: don't blame me, honey. I know your problem.

Then one morning it ended, because it had to end. She was gone. She has never come back.

But then, I haven't either. Or at least, such was my hope that went with her, as I stared at the frozen Green.

Turning from the memory, I got into the pickup with Zeke, my Labrador, and my shotgun. I had a desire to shoot a duck, kill something to lay as sort of a sacrifice on the altar of a tragicomic summer gone down. Pagan stuff, a necessary bloodletting perhaps. I didn't really feel like hunting, or think I'd get any birds this late in the fall. But because it would be my last chance, I had to try.

Behind me, the tires of the pickup made two black stripes in the fresh snow. Up in the stiffened aspen and sepulchers of lodgepole pine, I couldn't even see the bones of our big brisket steers. The snow had healed the land, and was banking and riffling across the ice-locked beaver ponds. I wondered if I could perhaps snag one final brook trout, or at least carry the vision of one through what I knew would be a long winter ahead. But the gates in the fences were open, the cattle and game gone. I drove the truck slowly along the river, resigned to the fact that I'd missed the ducks this year.

But Zeke, then, with his uncomplicated dog-mind, began whining next to me, his black nose pointing at a thumb of land jutting into the river. I stopped the truck and grabbed my binoculars. It was hard to see in the thick wet snowflakes dapping down. I don't think Zeke could possibly have seen, yet he'd whined, given mark to something. There, just off the point in the willows, where he and I had often shot, my lenses picked up at least half a dozen mallards. They were northern birds, with gleaming green heads, and pig-fat—some of these weigh about eight pounds—strangers, obviously, lighting in here not realizing that the locals had all departed.

We began sneaking, then, through the whitened, muffled sagebrush, down into russet-red willow thickets. My hands were so cold I had to keep blowing into them; even gloves couldn't ward off the wet chill. Zeke was excited with his find. I whispered him in to heel...we were belly-crawling now in the moose trails in the willows. Snow stuffed the barrels of my 12-gauge; I'd have to pick it out and Zeke would slither away from me, sniffing the last few yards toward the river. Suddenly, snow showered off the willows to my right; in a crashing explosion, something black with yellow legs: a bull moose erupted from where he'd been sleeping, a few feet from me. As I recoiled, not wanting to get in the road of this thundering beast, a cow moose sprang at me from the other side, and she was followed by a yearling, probably her calf from the year before. I'd interrupted a family breed-in. All three of them swept past me in angry grunts, baring their teeth. They went directly to my left, leaping the last few yards, snapping off willows as they plunged down the four-foot-high bank and splatted into the river.

"Dammit!" I shouted, slipping to get up in the snow, Zeke spinning around me in frantic circles. I jerked my gunbarrel at him: "Come back here. The birds are all gone now."

They were indeed; twelve superb mallards were quacking up in the gray scud sky. By the time I saw them they were a good seventy yards off; no possible shot, nor would they be returning to this sheltered and last unfrozen pool beside the point. The moose had swum right through it, cracking the surrounding ice in snorting echoes, then slogging up onto the other bank where they shook themselves and steamed and sneered at me for interrupting their idyll.

I sighed. Well, goodbye duck season. "Let's go," I murmured to Zeke, and upright, abandoning Indian-style, I started slogging back toward the truck. But Zeke was half crouching just a few yards away, where he could see down below the bank. He was shivering, which was strange, because he hadn't yet been in the water. I thought maybe he'd hurt himself, so I brushed through the last willow screen and came up to him.

What he was looking at was a Canada goose, about six feet away, beady eyes blinking at me, the tall neck lifting. Goose? The wariest of all the birds, the prize? What was a goose doing in the midst of swearing and crashing and swimming beasts? Sleeping, that's what! And in his awakening and mine, a giant unfolding consternation began slapping the bank, honking to a thunder of wings, one, three, seven . . . I lost count. A gaggle of geese, twenty or thirty at least, sprang into flight not ten feet below me, down the sharp bank where they'd all been asleep on a spit of sand.

My hands were frozen, my arms didn't work. WHOOM! Something fired the gun between my hip and shoulder; it almost blasted out of my grasp. And there were feathers and goose droppings pelleting into the black unfrozen pool; great gouting, beating wings soaring upward toward the moose across the river, who were watching too. Zeke was splashing out into the river. Of couse I had a bird down; he was paddling madly after something. My gun barrel swept up. Double, triple, get 'em all. I fanned the sight across the arching gray column. WHOOM! Now Zeke was swimming further out in the river, clawing up onto the ice. Got something in his mouth. He turned leaped off back toward shore. Around a nub of frozen earth, screened from me, four more geese were running on the water, slapping their wingtips. They rose into flight, I reaching into my pocket, pulling out pipes, a glove, shells, which spilled into the willows. Stuffed two into the gun! Why the hell didn't they fit? Snapped it finally shut, lifted it up. Nothing but gray misting snow, and the sound of all of them, hidden in it, beating away.

"Where are my birds?" I cried. "Fetch, Zeke, fetch!"

Zeke lay panting on the sandbar. Then, wearily, he pushed up, scaled the river bank, and came close enough to me so that when he shook himself, I caught the full spray of icy droplets: his tears and mine. I stood watching the river until the last ripples in the black pool stilled, and the fallen goose feathers began to freeze into the ice. Even the moose had trudged away.

Every bird was gone. I'd never touched one!

Right then, a strange thing happened. It took a moment or two for the shock of losing to wear off. But after it did, I found myself standing in the snow with the flakes melting on my face. I was laughing. The mighty hunter, eh? And what had I hoped to get? A goose, two or three. Dead, cold carcasses, symbols of the win.

And for what? That was the point. None of us particularly liked to eat goose. The meat was usually tough, and furthermore, Teddy insisted that they mated for life. When I'd carry the carcasses home, she'd almost weep for the widows or widowers I'd left behind. Why do you have to do it? she'd plead.

In that moment, I began realizing that I didn't have to. I even think that the reflexes of my eye and hand were aware of the change before I was. Something in me wanted me to miss those geese, as if a voice within were crying out: you don't need them to eat, and least of all as a trophy.

But what then? I wanted to shout back. Has all my effort, my belly-crawling stalk, been only a stroll in the snow?

Of course! the voice cried. What else is there? The beauty of the moment—hasn't your blessing been to connect with it, to live it? Isn't your trying, your caring, all the reward you'll ever need?

I walked back to the truck, still smiling. "Don't worry, Zeke," I said as he hopped in, "there'll be quail in Arizona before long." He glanced up at me with muddy eyes of doubt. But for a gooseless hunter it seemed enough. On the strength of it, we headed south.

It's a long, hard drive from Wyoming to Arizona. Eleven hundred miles, two numbing days. As many times as I've made the trip, I prefer to do it alone. Because, in a sense, it's like a retreat, a time of total silence in which the great majesty of the American West wraps itself around me, and my track through it seems joined to all the wagon roads of other wanderers who had come this way.

Now, with Zeke and Mamma cat as my only company,

I searched for the lonely Utah highway where I'd taught Tom to drive when we'd made our first trip up from California. Here, too, in the Wasatch mountains was the long canyon where John, years before, had crawled into the front seat beside me and picked up my ukelele. He'd strum it, and frown as he struggled to learn the fingering. I'd reach over and show him the chords of C and F, which were the only keys I could play. It seemed hard to believe that from these beginnings in the mountains, John had become an accomplished musician. Alternating between piano and guitar, he led his own band at Stanford. Teddy and I had listened with pride the night that John and his group opened a two-week engagement in a Reno hotel. The Heavenly Days, they called themselves.

Their songs seemed to follow me down the trail to the south, the memories of the picnics we'd had up at the beaver ponds in Wyoming, dozens of young friends around a campfire, John and Pete plucking guitars, and Tom playing his drums with tinny spoons on Dutch ovens.

When the kids were finally gone, back to make their own worlds far from the ranches, Teddy and I felt no void in our lives. There was no time to remain as fixed and clinging parents, because we had new challenges now in the land, and the slow unfolding growth that Nature demanded of us as its herdsmen. I must admit, however, one moment of mourning. When Peter, our youngest, finally left us I simply took my bird dog, went over to a marsh in the sagebrush and wept. But that did it. End of an era.

So now, racing across the ocher flats of northern Arizona, I glanced at Zeke and Mamma cat. Their heavy-lidded eyes were watching me. I reached over, stroked Zeke's head, and smiled. Substitute children, no doubt, but I have heard that it reduces blood pressure when man touches animals. Because he's spent so many millennia with them, they're part of him. I have no way of knowing if the theory is correct. My blood pressure has never been high.

As I finally reached the Arizona mountains, those massive black temples above Phoenix, I remembered a Buddhist book I'd glanced at sleepily the night before. The last line had read: "A peaceful life is to forget yourself completely and be what you are."

3

Fall of the Masked Bobwhite

"You might not like it," the young man warned me. "It's a long dusty road."

"Well, I've been down a few of those."

"All right. Meet you at your mail box on the Sasabe highway, five A.M."

So began another search. The next morning in the still-sultry heat of October, the young man drove me to Mexico. Though the side of his truck was stenciled "U.S. Government," Roy Tomlinson looked anything but official. He wore a beard and casual khakis, and the back of his Travelall was loaded with bird feed, traps, and tape recorders. Once, in fact, when Tomlinson had inadvertently run a roadblock in the darkened desert, the Mexican Federal Judicial Police had thrust machine pistols into his face. They were convinced he was a drug smuggler. Only through fast talking and verification of his U.S. government ID card would they let him go.

He was a biologist with the U.S. Fish and Wildlife Service. What had brought us together was his particular assignment for the Endangered Species Bureau: find and preserve the Sonoran masked bobwhite quail.

As we drove down the sandy cattle trail that served as a road below Sasabe, Tomlinson fascinated me with the story of the masked bobwhite. When the conquistadores and padres came to the Altar Valley in the mid-1700s, with typical Spanish thoroughness they uncovered a uniquely curious bird. They had already observed, of course, the profusion of quail in the Sonoran desert: the bluish, topknotted ones that later were named Gambel; also the *perdis*, or slightly larger mountain quail high up the rocky canyons; and the usually enormous coveys of a gray quail with a white topknot, known as the Scaled, because of the patterning of his feathers.

But nowhere in the Spanish world had the explorers ever come on anything as bizarre as this new Sonora breed. He seemed almost an imposter, for his breast was as orange-red as a robin's, his back a brown-whitish camouflage similar to bobwhite quail in the eastern U.S. And, as if ashamed of the whole combination, Nature had chosen to hide this little fellow's face behind a black mask. The idea of the mask must have appealed to Spanish taste, perhaps evoking romantic memories of *gran bailes* in Seville or Cadiz. At any rate, the explorers were profuse in their admiration for this bird. They noted that he refused to live with the commoner quail out in the rocky desert. Instead, he chose the rich, swaying grasslands of the lower lomas or slopes. And he was particularly choosy about his mating habits. Unless the grassland was drenched with summer rain, he refused to breed.

As Roy Tomlinson pointed out, the masked bobwhite was ill equipped for the "progress" that the conquistadores could never dream lay ahead. The birds' original range had been an elongated egg, the north end containing certain high grassland valleys in the Tucson area, and extending south through similar terrain about a hundred miles into Sonora. In the early years, the Apache and other warlike Indian cultures had kept the birds alive, simply by driving from the region anything but a rudimentary Spanish culture. But with the slow extermination of the Apaches after the U.S. Civil War, settlers swarmed into southern Arizona: soldiers, miners, cattlemen, and finally sun seekers. As desert towns began to sprawl out, the old grasslands were devoured by reservoirs, and slag dumps of mines. What remained of the more remote grasslands were then incorporated into far more efficient ranching operations than the earlier Spanish grants on whose lands they were based. Texas cattlemen, lured by a sea of grass on the lomas, moved in with thousands of animals, peeling the tender gramas year after year. Permanent spring-fed steams slowly dried up. Topsoil was replaced by hardpan, and when the rains struck now, they scourged the lands with muddy flash floods and deep-cut arroyos, sweeping away the quail nests and their shelter from prey. Where there had once been grass, there were now burroweed and an infestation of scrubby mesquite trees, devouring whatever water was left.

When the last Sonoran masked bobwhite disappeared from Arizona in the early 1900s, some biologists felt that the species had been wiped from the face of the earth. But generations of pioneer ecologists kept searching for them, and through the efforts of these men and Roy Tomlinson, driving miles of dusty roads, a handful of the birds were finally located on an isolated ranch in Sonora. But they wouldn't be here long. Progress was threatening even this remote grassland. The Mexican who owned the ranch was already beginning to rip and farm his fields, which would be the deathknell of the last few coveys.

By late morning, Tomlinson and I had reached the ranch. It reminded me of the "El Silencios," the great silent ranchos where I used to buy my Mexican corrientes in the palmy pre-Okie days. Lying in a wildness of coppery mountains were pastures thousands of hectares in size. They were already streaked with arroyos where strings of greening mesquite attested to overgrazing and the woody climax beginning.

As we drove through a last remaining yellowy bottom-land of grass, Tomlinson said nervously: "As hot as it is, midday now, we're going to be lucky to find any birds." But he stopped shortly along a brush-filled arroyo, and placed his tape recorder on the truck's hood. For a long time, the two of us stood in the sun, hearing an eerie cacaphony of quail calls spooling out. Peeps, clucks, food and danger signals. Finally Tomlinson shook his head, and unleashed his lemon and white springer spaniel. "They're just not answering," he said, "so we'll have to walk for 'em. Dammit, I know they're here someplace—if some bastard hasn't come in and trapped 'em."

Though neither of us had a gun in our hands, I'd never felt as excited as I did in that moment, watching the little dog shudder through the brush, her tail quivering, then freezing.

"Now!" Roy cried. Out they exploded, first one, with a strange little cry, then more, breasts orange in the sun. They leaped up exactly as did eastern bobwhite, which I'd hunted as a boy. They were strong fliers, healthy birds, and when they took cover a short distance away, their black faces would flash as if mocking: watch us now; we can hide better than you desert people know how to hunt.

Well, they did hide from us, and we left it at that. We'd seen what we came for. "They *do* exist," Tomlinson said, "and this is our number-one program at the bureau now. We're going to make these birds live again in Arizona, or damn well find the reason why."

As we drove north that night, he outlined the program the bureau had in mind. "Your ranch," he explained, "still has some original grassland, decaying yes, but not totally abused. We think it's the habitat. We're prepared to take environmental control of those pastures, set up bird pens and living facilities for a resident biologist. You will be denied any cattle grazing or agricultural income from the land. However, we'll pay you what we consider an adequate wildlife lease, on a long-term basis. If you'd like to help on the project, does that have any appeal?"

I felt like saying, I thought you'd never ask! Before the night was done, in the kitchen of the Las Delicias adobe, we'd worked out the rudiments of a plan. Teddy and I were overjoyed. In our hopes for this little masked bird, no deus ex machina could have ever flown into our coop at a more opportune moment!

That fall, we'd reached a time of taking stock. If there was to be any centering in our lives, reality demanded that we look at where we were, and where we wanted to go— and chop down any dead timber between.

Though Teddy's fatigue, as predicted by her doctor, was a gnawing worry, her recovery did seem to be proceeding. The summer of the Okies was behind us now, and we were delighted to leave it as a bad dream, fading away.

I could not, however, say the same for the economic recovery of the ranch. Thus, when my partner came up to the house late one afternoon, I knew we were playing out a last sad scene. But he proved to be just what he was, an honest man. He urged that we keep the feedlot going; sure, we'd taken a hard shot, a loss, but we could eat our way out of it. We'd built a good team of kids in our workers, and didn't want to let them down. The cattle market was bound to turn around, once the disaster of the Nixon price freeze had been digested.

Somewhere in those dusk hours, over the ledger books, I seemed to remember my father telling me, never duck bad news. It won't go away. Get it over with as quickly as you can.

So I told my partner, we bite the bullet. I was through, the ranch was through. Let the good kids go, including my brother-in-law, young hero Bill. Junk off what we had, and pay our debts.

We did just that, and more, unfortunately. In the drought of the summer, I'd ended up with a ranch that was, as cowmen say, "peeled," a parking lot of dust. I'd also sold most of my good cows, to gamble on the feedlot, so now I'd have to reach into the sock again and buy other cows. The expenses of a ranch run on: you have to cover them, grass or no grass. After the feedlot was gutted and the machines hauled away, I had a shambles on my hands, a massive livestock scale and new corrals, all of which I had to repurchase from the defunct feedlot company, to help pay off the bank. With each check written, I winced and lashed out for solutions: level the entire feedlot complex, scorch the earth to desert so I wouldn't have to pay taxes on it, let alone look at it. No, better yet, split it off from the ranch: sell the several hundred acres of wells and fields.

About then, I was approached by a neighbor who owned massive cattle ranches. He waited for bargains like this. But as we began to bargain, his enthusiasm seemed to wane. He told me frankly, "Your tenants wrecked this place. It's worth very damn little now." However, he might just make an offer on it, throw me a life jacket. It was exactly this prospect that I'd been bleakly debating when Roy Tomlinson had driven me down the dusty road to the masked bobwhite.

Within a few weeks, the Fish and Wildlife contract had reached my desk. The lease was frugal, and would restrict our use of three square miles of good grazing in the center of the ranch. No cowman in his right mind would have wanted to sign it. On the other hand, I was less a cowman now, and enjoying it more. Leasing the land meant I didn't have to go to the expense of stocking it. And the thought of raising animals to live rather than die was infinitely appealing. "But can we afford to do it?" Teddy asked nervously.

I answered that we were going to do it, and worry about the "can" later. That same night, I telephoned my neighbor and told him the feedlot was no longer for sale. When I said we were turning it over to the birds, he responded with a rather curious "hmmmm."

Through a stroke of good furtune, about the time Roy Tomlinson had approached us with the quail project, an ethnologist friend from the University of Arizona had asked permission to make an artifacts survey of the Las Delicias. When I agreed eagerly, because I've always been fascinated by anything to do with American Indians, two graduate anthropologists reported for duty. They were strapping young girls who'd take to the mesquite armed with trowels and gridded maps. In the sandy arroyos of the Las Delicias, relatively untouched by pothunters, the young ladies hoped to establish proof that the Hohokam culture had existed here simultaneously with the later Pima-Papago. As I was to learn, the apparently superior Hohokam people had once occupied all of this region of the Sonoran Desert. But then, about 1450, in a sudden termination that still has the anthropologists speculating, the Hohokam vanished and there was a gap of several hundred years before the Piman peoples took over. Had a plague, drought, or genocide struck the Hohokam? Or could they have migrated to become the Pueblo-dwellers of northern Arizona? No one could say, and it was exactly this mystery that appealed to my romanticism. Even when I hunted quail now, I often paused to pick up fragments of old pots.

We had some tantalizing clues. Petroglyphs, pecked into the rocks of the Las Delicias canyons, had been carbon-dated to at least A.D. 800. So they were clearly Hohokam messages. Often I'd studied these strange marks; photographed and painted them. But nobody knew what they meant. The earliest ones were primitive renditions of coiled serpents, lizards, or an occasional bird. The more recent glyphs included stick figures, as if the natives were becoming conscious of themselves in the environment. The drawings appeared in clusters, pecked into lichen-covered rocks at the mouths of the canyons. From such vantage points, the Indians could watch the long mesquite slopes below, either for game or approaching marauders. One of the anthropologists felt that the petroglyphs were no more than Indian doodling, some tribal group passing the time until the rains would come. Then they'd go down into the desert and make dams in the arroyos, diverting the water for their primitive systems of agriculture.

Old Bartolomeo, my Mexican cowboy, had a simpler explanation for the petroglyphs. "Limite de terreno," he called them—a boundary of land. A particular family group or clan, he explained, probably chose to identify themselves as the Snakes or the Hawks. When they'd camp at the mouth of a canyon, they'd "mark it" with their sign, thus reserving this place as their clan's hunting ground. Because Bartolomeo clearly had an Indian face, and could locate water with a divining stick of green mesquite, I set greater store by his theory than those of the city anthropologists.

In fact, it was Bartolomeo who got me in trouble with

the university ladies. The doughty girls, in their meticulous grid-mapping, had located what appeared to be an old Indian town in the San Miguel pasture. They showed me streaks of hardpan clay that had undoubtedly been walls of dwellings. I asked the girls when we were going to dig it up, but at that point they were interested more in pure science than in pickaxe work. Eventually, my curiosity overcame me. One afternoon when Bartolomeo and I were out looking for cattle, we rode past the streaks in the clay. I'd already been whacking into them with a wrecking bar, but it was like pounding pure concrete. Bartolomeo's eyes gleamed. "Ah, señor," he said, "por que no el gato?"

El gato indeed, and it went right to the heart of the matter. We had an old yellow crawler tractor that was surplus from the feedlot. Within an hour, I'd fired it up and come clunking out to dig a swatch through the Indian wall. The first thing I hit was a nest of rattlesnakes. As the tracks flung them up, they came slithering toward the seat, Bartolomeo crying: "Cuidado, cuidado!" But after the snakes had wriggled away, and the pack rats with them, we struck paydirt. Several metates—grinding stones— came out intact, and with them much large and decorative pottery. Bartolomeo was overjoyed. We'd beaten the earth, made a haul. But when I later confessed what I'd done, the anthropologists were aghast. They ordered me to go back and bury my trove at once. Sheepishly, I did so, scoop by scoop. Even Bartolomeo had shrugged philosophically. "Mejor," he said. "Quisas los indios no gustan." Maybe the Indians wouldn't like it, and maybe he was right. After that little foray, whenever I'd find a piece of a pot, I'd turn it over, admire it, and drop it again into the sand.

But out of my diggings that fall, regardless of how clumsy and amateurish, there did come a slow sense of rootedness into the earth here. And a humbling, too, as I found myself sharing the primitive rhythms of a vanishing race. As the Papago saying goes: "Let me walk in the way of the fox, so that the earth will never know that my footprint has been upon it."

Now certainly I couldn't be an Indian, didn't want to be, yet for most of my life I'd been drawn toward them, as if instinctively I wanted to understand them better, perhaps as the dark, hidden side of my own spirit. But the process had been slow and often exasperating.

When we first began spending winters on the Arizona ranch, we quickly realized how different it was from the challenges we'd faced in Wyoming. Up there, though the people strode around in boots and had a fierce independence, you could still get a straight yes or no answer, and usually from somebody who had a Scotch-Irish name. But down in the Altar Valley of the Las Delicias, we found ourselves surrounded by Mexican cowboys on all the ranches, thinking, speaking, and dying for their culture, not ours. And to the west were the Papago Indians, whose sprawling reservation was the size of Connecticut and abutted almost to the tops of our canyons. When the Papagos felt an urge to break out into civilization, their first watering place (beer drinking and peeing, both) was a trading post just north of the ranch.

Here, one afternoon, I happened to talk with a nicely dressed Papago. We discussed cattle prices and some Indian baskets that were for sale. He'd obviously spent time in the military because his hair was cut short and he spoke English, with a few traces of GI slang. After I'd bought the supplies I'd come for, and gone outside, the pleasant young Papago beckoned at me. "Sir" he said— he was now in the company of two hulking Papago braves with shoulder-length hair—"how about lending me a dollar?"

I sighed. I almost knew it was coming, but was disappointed that it had. I asked him if he had a job, and he said yes, he worked for the Bureau of Indian Affairs. In that case, I said, it would be demeaning for him to accept money from me. We would lose respect for each other, and a possible friendship. While I was waxing philosophic, he kept nodding pleasantly, saying: "Yessir, that's absolutely right. Never thought of it that way." And when my lecture was done, he added, "Then how about fifty cents?"

A few days later, I recounted the incident to a Franciscan priest who'd served for years out on the Papago Reservation. How, I asked, could the Papago, when he seemed in total agreement with what I was saying, come back with such a baldfaced request?

The priest chuckled. "Simple. He knew you had money, so therefore you knew how to get more. Since he didn't know how to get more, he figured you'd share with him what you had. All Indians do that. It's a mark of a man's greatness, how much he gives away."

Much of the charm that seemed born into our neighboring Papagos sprang from their insouciance and splendid directness. In the days before Refugia had graced our kitchen, one of the many "mothers' helpers" that Teddy had tried was a Papago woman, Maude. Eventually, during Maude's on-again-off-again employment, several of her many children came to live with us. They were delightful kids whom we immediately fell in love with. I was always buying them ball mitts or dice games, and one night I brought home from the trading post an Indian dance record. They call their music "chicken scratch," a quick-step sort of polka, hybridized with Mexican and Indian strains. To amuse young Robert and his beautiful sister, Magdalen, who was about ten, I began twirling Teddy around the kitchen. Magdalen watched us for several moments. Then, with a saucy shake of her head, she sprang up and literally snatched me away from Teddy. "Here, white man," she cried, "I show you how to chicken scratch!" Erect and proud, she clapped her little body against mine and whirled me away, not hesitating to kick my feet when I made a wrong step.

Her mother, Maude, who watched us and chuckled, was probably the happiest, most carefree woman I've ever known. There was no way to make her sulk or mourn. She always saw the comic side of everything, with good reason perhaps. Shortly after spending her menstrual rite in a mud hut—which she described in richer detail than I needed—she'd apparently gone on to serial pregnancies, interrupted only by nuns at a Phoenix boarding school teaching her to be a lady. She did learn a beautiful, cursive handwriting, but the triumphs of parochial education ended there.

When she'd get sick from alcohol, which was as often as she could find it, she'd either wreck her car, break a limb, or drift back to the reservation with her face pulped and her eyes blackened, and end up being restored by one of the local medicine men. Maude had had at least eight children of record, though not necessarily by the same fathers. For a woman who must have weighed two hundred pounds and was as wide as an ax handle across the beam, she had an amazing number of boyfriends.

For instance, after one of the many times she'd gotten drunk and quit us, she returned lovingly to the ranch with two of her suitors, insisting on showing them the kitchen where she'd spent so many happy days. These Indians were nice, big fellows, prominent in the tribe, she said, and between them and her, they polished off eight beers in no more than ten minutes. By now, Maude was on a crying jag as she went pirouetting around the kitchen, showing her cook routine to the fellas, and alternately hugging Teddy and saying how much she loved her. "Oh," she cried, "I've been so happy here! Do you know what I miss the most?"

"What, Maude?" Teddy asked, as if uncertain whether it was her or simply the new electric stove.

"Artichokes!"

"Artichokes!" roared the men. They leaned back in their chairs, slapped the table, and guffawed until you could have heard it all the way to the reservation. And why was the eating of artichokes so funny? Damned if I know, and never will.

What was not so funny, however, was Maude's final, final evening with us. About nine o'clock, I was over in my adobe office, pecking something on my typewriter when the door banged open. "Indios! Muchos!" cried Bartolomeo, who, despite his own mixed ancestry, was terrified of pure Indians. Then, switching to Mexican-English in his excitement, he rattled: "Bad hombres, they come by my house, wake me up, then go out in the shop, playing around with la gordita's car!"

That would be the junker we'd recently bought for Maude. We'd put it in the shop for safekeeping so she couldn't wreck it again until she'd at least worked the payments down a little more. As I hurried with Bartolomeo out into the desert darkness, we ran smack into five Indians, skulking along the edge of the patio by Maude's room. They wore headbands around their shoulder-length hair; at least two spoke no English. But what astonished me was that these were all youths, certainly not half Maude's age. On the other hand, we'd recently added to our entourage, in addition to Maude's younger children, another of her daughters, the lissome, seventeenish Ruth. She was such a pretty girl that when I once took her to Tucson, helping her look for a job, a prunish waitress in a diner gave me a dirty-old-man look and refused to serve us.

Well, clearly, the young raiding party had swarmed down on us to snatch Ruth. But not at all, Teddy said as she emerged from the "Indian wing" of the adobe. Behind her, in the dimly lit bathroom, I could see powder puffs flapping and warpaint going on. What had happened, Teddy explained, was that the boys had come by, and wanted to take Ruth *and* Maude in Maude's (our) car out on a harmless little date, down to the border town of Sasabe, twenty miles away.

"Harmless?" I echoed. Sasabe at this hour of night was just one beer-slopped saloon. "You let her go with them," I warned, "and it's curtains." Another wreck, and goodbye artichokes.

"But," Teddy kept saying, "she's a grown woman, and we can't really stop her, can we?"

At that moment Maude emerged, powdered and perfumed like a circus elephant, and Ruth mincing behind her on high heels and dangling a glittering little purse. "We just be gone an hour or so with the fellas," Maude beamed. "And they gonna pay you for the gas too, okay?"

Okay. Sure. Hoka hey, as the Sioux say. A great day to die.

Of course nobody died. Sometime far into the dawn, they all swarmed back to the ranch, two of the braves sleeping it off under mesquite trees, and the other luckier fellows ending up with the squaws. All that really came out of that night was nine months, followed by babies— one for Ruth, her second out of wedlock—and, yes, still another for poor Maude, who certainly didn't need *that* experience again!

The morning after, wreathed in smiles and a hangover, Maude heaped her three kids and five braves into her junker car, which looked like a circus stationwagon, and neither she nor our mortgage has ever been heard of since.

We did, however, manage to get one last glimpse of daughter Ruth. Months later, through some vague desert telegraph, we'd heard a rumor that she was alive, pregnant, and living in a shack out on the reservation. Teddy and I had decided to spend a couple of days down on the beach in Mexico. To get there, we had to drive through the Papago lands, and at the prospect of this, Teddy's eyes gleamed.

In our tribe's hasty departure from the ranch, Teddy realized that they had forgotten not only the baseball mitts and dice games, but, more important, a big bundle of presents. The fact that Christmas was only a couple of weeks away made it mandatory that we deliver the goods, and our trip to the beach was a perfect excuse.

There turned out to be only one problem with our Santa Claus mission: when we reached the little house in Papagoland, it appeared forlorn and abandoned. I spent a few minutes wandering around the other adobes, asking the neighbors, but, as often with Papagos, they would only shrug or pretend they'd never heard of Maude and her brood. I tried to persuade Teddy that we simply ought to open the door and dump the stuff, but she would hear none of it. In this case, Santa would hand-carry or else—and I must say I wanted to get one more grin from those wonderful, black-haired kids.

Several days later, en route back from the beach we pulled into the little Indian village again. Standing in front of the house was Ruth, her pretty blue squaw dress not quite hiding her tummy. The younger kids were at school, but Ruth promised to give them their share of the booty. Unlike the beery, ebullient Maude, Ruth didn't show emotion easily, yet she was clearly touched by our thought. We'd taken a special interest in Ruth's future, and her mother had brought her to us hoping that we might give Ruth opportunities she couldn't have on the reservation. Because Ruth could type about as fast as a turtle, and seemed determined to become a secretary, Teddy had repeatedly made hundred-mile trips into Tucson, hauling her to employment agencies and job contacts we had set up by leaning on any friend we could. Teddy had bought Ruth typing books and spent hours with her over homework, teaching her to increase her speed. And then, just on the eve of getting a job and breaking out finally, what did she do but blow it all away!

Ruth was nodding glumly, sighing, and finally whispering that she was sorry. But we didn't come for sorry. "Ruth," Teddy pleaded, "you're bright, you're pretty—you have such great promise. You don't have to live this way. If you believe in yourself, discipline yourself, you can rise above it, don't you see?"

Great, I thought. The sermon was almost over. Dump the trade goods and let's go. Just at that moment, I happened to glance away from mournful Ruth. In a bean patch behind the shack, I saw a young Indian in Levi's raise a shovel and drive it like a spear into the earth. Well, I thought, there were a lot of Indians around, performing shadowy ranch chores in the mesquite. But this one was now coming toward us with fists balled and a face dark with anger. At that moment, a brooding shadow crossed my memory. A fellow named Rinaldo. Once in a while, furtively, Ruth or Maude had mentioned him. Yes, it was admitted that Rinaldo fathered Ruth's first illegitimate child. But then there was a gap and nobody spoke much of Rinaldo. Where Rinaldo had been, I was to learn, was in prison, for carving on another young Papago with a knife. Now, this sunny morning, here he came, just released from the cooler, and determined to guard his squaw from the predations of the palefaces.

In he swept like a desert thunderstorm, kicking up dust; and with his chest puffed out, Rinaldo shoved himself between Teddy and Ruth. Teddy was still engrossed in the spiritual aspects of Ruth's behavior. But what I was reading was only the thunder in Rinaldo's face. I whispered, "Daaa-rling," as if she hadn't seen him. And then I was slinking onto the seat of the car, reaching under it, hoping I still had my .38 revolver down there someplace—my precaution for Mexico that might come in handy here, should push come to shove.

At that moment, to my horror, Teddy not only saw Rinaldo but punched her finger right into his chest.

"If you're going to make Ruth your wife," she cried, "and take charge of this new baby of hers, then what I'm telling her goes for you as well. You don't have to let yourselves rot out. You're young, you've got futures ahead of you if you'll just take them. Now, pull yourselves together and do something about it!"

Rinaldo was speechless. Even his heavy lids had peeled back to expose eyes. Then rank fury tightened his jaw. His fist raised as if he were going to pound Teddy like a fence post.

"Yes, you, Rinaldo!" She jabbed him again in the chest. "You can *be* something if you want. Now you just grow up and...and stop acting like a damn drunken Indian!"

Ow! The arrow in the heart. As I cringed there, hearing that awful echo, I could think only of the graves of all those Franciscans and Jesuits, scattered across the desert, for giving their sermons to the indigent natives. Yet, the ghosts of the departed fathers must have been beaming down on Teddy. To my amazement, Rinaldo's murderous glower gave way slowly to an astonished gape until, with one last tentative kick at the dust he shrugged and grudged off into the shade of the house. Ruth was sniffling now. Teddy hugged her and I slid the toys onto the front step like a badly battered peace pipe. As we drove away and left them standing there, mutely staring at us, I breathed to Teddy: "I have to hand it to you, you sure pulled that one out of the fire!"

"And for what? She hasn't got a chance, the poor little thing. God help her."

Well, they were gone now, "our Indians," and yet that fall as I dug for the artifacts of their ancestors, I felt a sense of the nobility of these people. Their tragedy had been that they were what they were. It was we who demanded that they change, to become "us." For three hundred years they had suffered our devastating culture, but now, some of them seemed to be transcending it toward a more hopeful future. And the path they were taking was a return not to our mode but to their own: their authentic "Indianness."

Strong tribes like the Sioux, Navajo, and Apache were clearly showing a pride in their nationhood: Indian lands for Indian people, Indian self-financing enterprises, without whites and one day, they hoped, without the demeaning dole of government and outside meddlers. When I once asked a Papago what was the average size of their families, he grinned and said, "Mother, father, five kids— and one social worker."

Ours was a world they'd never made, and yet, in their hopeful return to their own, I could only wish them Godspeed. We were all inching on the same road.

The immediate problem on the ranch that fall was management. With the demise of the feedlot, our Vietnam vets had moved on to steadier work. Even Bill Kent, the family soldier of fortune, was beginning a new ranching life on his own, hiring out to clear jungles in Ecuador. Though the masked bobwhite program was utilizing some of our pastures, Teddy and I still had several hundred cows, with which we hoped to pay the operating costs.

Only loyal old Bartolomeo had stayed with us through the transition. Because he was in his late seventies, we'd hired him a compadre, Cosme, an excellent mountain cowboy who had the classic features of a Mexican with distinct Indian blood. Yaqui, we supposed, though it was a subject never discussed. Nor, or course, did anyone ever mention "macho."

Now, if there's one word that a rancher in the Southwest has to understand, *macho* is it. To be sure, I'd known a lot of fair-skinned Anglo cowboys from Montana to California who were confirmed macho-trippers with their feisty swagger, because such is the traditional ethic of the West. But they could all take lessons from the Mexican, particularly those with high proportions of Indian in their blood. Because, mingled with it in the Mexican are the tightlipped Spanish codes of honor, loyalty, shame, and vengeance. The bouquet of this blend is "machismo"—maleness, bravery, and self-proving often to the point of idiocy.

Yet, managing macho is a necessity if you hope to operate a ranch in a hostile desert that only the Mexican seems equipped to stand. Somewhere along the line, it was the pride and sense of responsibility of the Bartolomeos and Cosmes that had built most of the great southwestern cattle empires.

Even at Bartolomeo's advanced age, he was as spry and indomitable as many forty-year-olds in the north country—and could rope a helluva lot better, with good reason! When Bartolomeo had just turned eleven, his father shoved him on a horse, pointed him into the Santa Rita mountains, and told him he was to lasso any wild cow running on those perilous, eight-thousand-foot slopes. These were feral animals with giant horns and not a brand on their hides. Few of them had ever seen a man. Bartolomeo's job was to rope the violent beasts, and tie each one to a burro that would lead them down the mountain.

Small wonder that by the time Bartolomeo was a young cowboy in his twenties, he'd developed a particularly macho idea about the kind of horseflesh he wanted under him. He used to delight in telling me about a colt that had once run away with him. After four stampeding miles, the colt slammed Bartolomeo into a barbed-wire fence, knocked him unconscious and broke his hand. "Don't worry," Bartolomeo said to me, "I teach him a lesson."

I'm always curious to get horsebreaking tips from these old timers, so I suggested that perhaps he had used a wire or chain noseband on the colt from then on.

Bartolomeo's Indian eyes smoldered. No, he said, what he'd done was to lead the colt into an arroyo, take off his saddle, and shoot him dead. "He don't run away ever again," and then Bartolomeo chuckled, as if enjoying the memory of how he had to walk the four miles back to the ranch house, lugging his heavy saddle.

Brutal? Yes, in our terms. And often senseless, as I was to find out that fall.

We'd scheduled a roundup, which would consist of moving several hundred cows and calves down out of rocky San Miguel canyon. Well, neither Bartolomeo nor Cosme was very pleased at having a *dama*, Teddy, along. Mexican women are never permitted within sight of a cow. But, because the señor was considered pretty much a gringo play-cowboy, Bartolomeo and Cosme suggested a better idea. Teddy loved the mountains, so I should take her for a nice, dude-type ride high up to the rim of the canyon. We'd idle our way up there about daybreak, Meanwhile, unbeknownst to us, Bartolomeo and Cosme, who always knew exactly where the cattle were located, would slip out about four that morning, ride to San Miguel in the dark, and by the time the useless *patrones* appeared, they, the machos, would have all the cattle nicely assembled. Not only would their maleness be thus exhibited to the encroaching female, but, more important, their pride would be shown to me.

But a funny thing happened on the way to the plot. Sometime in the night, the weather changed. In the sudden coolness, the cattle left the flats where Bartolomeo and Cosme had expected them. Virtually the entire herd was up on the rim of the canyon. To the delight of Teddy and me, we had the challenge of knocking hundreds of cows out of the rocks ourselves, and came whooping and beaming down to the corral, immensely proud of our catch.

Bartolomeo and Cosme sat carved in their saddles, as rigid as obsidian sphinxes. Had scalping knives been around, I would have feared for our hair. A moment later, the inevitable happened. Teddy made a perfectly innocent mistake, accidentally cutting a few cows back from the corral. In a normal roundup, Bartolomeo and Cosme would have only chuckled at this, or given her a stern glance. But at this moment, with no other outlet for the monumental insult to their macho, they both were standing in their stirrups, having a shoutdown with the boss and wife. Teddy was speechless, and I somewhat like John Foster Dulles, begging for a strategy of containment, or at least for an understanding of the senseless explosion. It seemed incredible that Bartolomeo and Cosme, both of whom loved us and this ranch, were now determined to self-destruct just to vent their humiliation that we, not they, had rounded up the cattle.

Indeed, that night, when tempers had cooled, they came to me, separately, and begged me to fire them. Clearly, they were not wanted on the ranch, not needed now that they had done such a terrible thing.

"Damn right you did," I said, and then gave them each quite a lecture, to the effect: how would *they* feel if I had spoken like that to *their* wives! As they squatted by the corral like hot, ticking irons, steaming mortification, I found myself playing my countermachismo role, I now the wounded one, alone here with a wife just out of her sickbed, and too many cows. How could I possibly run this ranch if they were to leave me? Furthermore, what responsible vaquero of many years' experience, of great reputation would suddenly abandon a ranch and animals at a critical time, just because his feelings had been hurt like a little girl's? They stiffened. They were not *that!* And, in truth, maybe they loved this ranch because there was so much to do here. It was not being operated properly. Did I know, they glowered, how badly I was running the ranch? Mendicantly, I said, yes, I did. I would take pains to correct it. But I couldn't do it alone. Gruffly, they began grunting: well, maybe they wouldn't leave me. I had a lot to learn, verdad? Verdad, which I could only learn from them, of course, leading finally to *abrazos*, new vows of determination, and it was all over. They would consent to take us back as *patrones*, *despite* the awful shame we had caused them.

In the process of getting the ranch back on its feet, I had some horse-breaking to do. We couldn't afford to buy replacement horses, and after enough sad experiences I didn't want to anyway, having learned that the ones you raise are at least the devils you know. With the Las Delicias we'd inherited a pair of young, wild fillies, the ugliest of which Bartolomeo had named "Chistosa," meaning funny little one, or joke—a bad joke in my case. When I first started to ride "Chisty"—horses in the breaking period should have short names so you can curse them more easily—she seemed willing enough. But always in a sulky sort of way. I'd have to pet her on the neck before I could lead her, and pet her again before I could lope her. Her eyes would become red and she'd glower at me with latent man-anger that I knew had to explode someday. (It finally did, once breaking my rib and a while later almost my neck, but that's another story!)

We had work to do, and that's always the best antidote for surly young horses. After the macho roundup in San Miguel, we'd now begun pushing the cows into the lower desert pastures. One morning when we'd ended up a few head short, I went loping back on Chisty to find them. This particular pasture was several thousand acres in size, and heavily covered with mesquite, an impenetrable jungle of green trees and thorns. It's easy to miss cows shading up in such places.

I rode for a long time, Chisty in a sulk and sluffing her feet as if to ask, was this trip necessary? At length I spotted a young black cow. She had a wild look in her eye and bolted from me like a deer. I made a run or two at her, but Chisty was such a stumble-footed slug I knew I could never catch the cow. The best I could do was to get her headed toward the pasture gate where Teddy or Bartolomeo would pick her up.

Then I turned Chisty and went back to a wide sand arroyo I'd been searching, because it seemed a logical place for more malingerers. By now, Chisty's eyes had grown very red. She was so angry at the continuation of this boring work that she was kicking the sand instead of walking. Indeed, I was just getting ready to curse her or whup her with my spurs when suddenly she stopped. Her ears shot up; her body felt alive under me. She was balking at the edge of the arroyo. I'd kick her out of it; she'd take a step or two forward, but then always turn her head back, in the direction we'd already covered. Finally, when I tired of turning her, I simply gave her her head.

She whirled into a thicket of mesquite. Now this was a filly that not only was lazy-sulky but also had a real distaste for pushing her head into a nest of mesquite thorns and her legs into the tearing catclaw. But here she was, ducking, plowing ahead through the jungle for a good forty or fifty yards until she stopped short. Her ears perked up again. She was sniffing toward the shadow of a fallen mesquite and a mass of dead limbs against the arroyo bank. I looked where she did, but never saw anything until a tiny glint of white moved under the debris. I wheeled down from Chisty's back, took a step or two into the shadow. A wet, newborn calf lay here. He was as black as his mother, which I then realized was the cow I'd just been running.

Had I not seen that speck of his one white foot, I never would have noticed him. I would have bummed him, that is, removed his mother, and left him for the coyotes to finish.

The remedy, of course, was quickly to return his mother so she could give him the first essential milk that would get him on his feet. When I remounted Chisty, I was elated, and patted her neck. "Good girl," I said. "Damn your ugly hide if you didn't save us a calf!"

But how had she done it? That's what struck me as I rode away to bring back the calf's mother. Moments before, Chisty and I had ridden right past the spot where the calf lay totally hidden. She couldn't have seen it. Nor, I realized, could she have winded it, because the wind was blowing from us to the calf.

How then? What instinct had exploded Chisty out of her life-daze and forced her to fight her way back to show me that calf? I didn't know, except that she had given me one visible sign. Her ears had gone up. In Chisty's dumb animal brain, she seemed to be hearing the calf.

What a remarkable sensory feat, I thought. And yet, wasn't it possible that a human could do the same thing? In animals and often in earth-connected people like the Indians, there seemed to be a great center of silence which they jealously guarded, as if knowing that any intrusion here would cut them off from a vital life force. As Thoreau put it, this was the beat of the different drummer, the unique selfhood that sounded in all of us, if we could but listen for it.

One Friday afternoon, Teddy and I drove the twenty-two miles to Sasabe, Sonora. It was our nearest church, and the Sunday mass was definitely a movable feast, sometimes said on Friday, sometimes Saturday, and often not at all, depending on the peregrinations of the missionary priest.

Regardless, when we crossed the border and began clunking our oil pan on the rocky roads of Sasabe, any schedule soon became meaningless. There was a feeling of entering a time warp. Sasabe's scatter of adobes, crusted against barren hills, had an Old Testament look, unchanging for the millennia, women in black shawls shuffling along behind burros carrying water in leaking tin cans. Because the town *pozo* ("well") never worked properly, water was hoarded and sold dearly. But there was plenty of beer in town, and shaded cantinas that had horses tied in front of them. Occasionally the vaqueros would ride into the cantinas and make their cowponies dance clattering on the stone floors. It was not uncommon to see vaqueros swaggering down the dusty main street with revolvers on their hips. Though there were large old ranches surrounding the pueblo, the townspeople themselves had only a few scrawny cows, which rooted among beer bottles, old tires, and car bodies littered in the arroyos. There were several rock creches to La Virgen where the people would put flowers, and the cows would always eat them. Even the cemetery, ablaze with flowers and gleaming white statuary, had an iron fence around it, big enough to keep the cows out, but not the jackrabbits.

Once, when we'd taken two friends from Dublin to mass with us, the gentle Irishwoman looked at Sasabe and gasped. "But, Otis," she said, "this dreadful poverty, how do you permit it?"

It was difficult to explain to a foreigner that the prosperous and powerful United States could be stopped dead at a cyclone fence, beyond which you fell into the timeless suffering of the ages. But the irony was that U.S. culture had indeed penetrated Sasabe, in ways that our Irish friends perhaps hadn't noticed. Out in the arroyos, atop houses that were not much better than packing crates, rose glittering TV antennae. And beside the slouched little Mexican Customs adobe at the border were several wrecked airplanes, the Cessnas and Pipers of American drug smugglers who had tried to land somewhere out in the rocks. The Mexican authorities had hauled the shattered fuselages up here and put a warning sign on them to all good neighbors from the north: "Do Not Buy Risks."

But that Friday afternoon, all Teddy and I bought in Sasabe was some Mexican beer, which I dearly love, and several pounds of their coffee, which is either the best or the worst you can ever taste, depending on whether they grind garbonza beans into it on certain days. Then the churchbell began to sound. Women in mantillas, and kids, straggled out of the adobes, and other parishioners jigged up on cadaverous horses bridled with string. From the old Spanish ranches far back in the mesquite came pickups filled with pretty girls. Carefully they'd brush the dust from their tight, double-knit flared slacks, bless themselves, and enter. Because the church doors were always kept open, dogs wandered in and out, along with whimpering toddlers who appeared to have no parents and not much in the way of diapers. A few vaqueros came too and there was a palsied cripple who wasn't right in the head. I'd heard a rumor that he'd been wounded with Villa in the revolution. He always kept standing and murmuring throughout the mass.

The priest who ministered Sasabe was a big-nosed Irish missionary, a tall, stooped man with a blotchy red face. I was relieved that this particular afternoon he didn't give a sermon.

Since leaving the Boston of his youth, he'd spent all of his life in the tropics. He'd learned Spanish in Guatemala by attending grade school with the kids, towering over them in what must have been conspicuous embarrassment that never seemed to leave him. His Spanish was quavering, harsh, and always painful to listen to. He'd been sick most of his years, chronic dysenteries, malarial fevers out of the swamps of banana towns.

Exiled from his culture and mumbling his days away in forgotten parishes, he was no silver-tongued money raiser or bingo master. When he gave communion, his hand trembled so badly he often had to grip it with the other hand. Some in Sasabe whispered that the padre "took" a little too much; that's why his face was always red and shiny. Others explained that poor padre was continually having to use strong drugs to kill the *microbas* in his stomach. Whatever, his hand trembled even more this Friday, and when he gave the last blessing, he didn't pat the altar boys on the head as he usually did, or empty the few pesos in the collection basket which, he mentioned once, usually amounted to about sixty-eight cents. No, this time, he simply stood in his tall, stooped way, his palms on the altar. The church was quiet and shadowy. He said, in his unfinished Spanish: "I'm leaving you."

He mumbled something else. I could hardly hear it. Yes, it was the sickness. They were sending him somewhere for the sickness. "This is my last mass here. I hope you will have a priest. I don't know if you will."

His eyes were red-rimmed. He brushed at them. "I am going to miss you," he whispered. "You are good people. I am going to miss you very much."

He obviously couldn't continue. Through the branches of a palo verde outside the window, the last afterglow of dusk flickered over his silent, bent form. He stood uneasily as if he no longer knew what to do with his trembling hands.

There was not a sound. Of the fifty people in the church, no one moved. Finally, an old woman wearing carpet slippers clopped up the aisle and laid her head against his shoulder. He held her and patted her. Younger women came then, two of them, and undid his robes that he couldn't fumble off. They embraced him, some kissing his hand. The old Villista shuffled up stiff-legged, and knelt before him. Father put both of his hands on his head. Every one of those fifty people came up the aisle individually and embraced him without a word. A dog was sniffing around the altar when Teddy and I came. She wept quiet tears like the others, and I was grateful I wouldn't have to speak. It seemed to take an hour for the church to empty: during it, no one spoke. When the burros and trucks were finally gone, Father was kneeling in the shadows, his face in his hands.

Teddy and I drove away, awed by the simple piety we'd seen here. These people huddled in the dusk of Sasabe weren't even particularly close to the old priest who spoke to them in gringo Spanish and would never be one of them. So how then explain that incredible silence, the unashamed weeping? Their tears were genuine, and their lack of words a tongueless humility that they could never express the void they felt now in their hearts.

Felt! That was the sensation that leapt out at me. Physical. Those simple people of Sasabe were believing with their bodies, tears, embraces, touches. They couldn't intellectualize the event as I might have. They had none of the cold detachment of my culture's pride. Instead, theirs was a gut reaction, enabling them to sense that priest as more than a limited, aging man. They were literally seeing through him to the spirit in themselves, and hence the gnawing emptiness when they realized that their vital connection with God was being severed.

Thus when the red-faced padre would tremble out a parable, their faces would reflect the repose of certainty. "Look at the birds in the air," the padre would say in his excruciating Spanish: "They do not sow and reap and store in barns, yet their Heavenly Father feeds them. You are worth more than the birds! Set your mind on God's kingdom and justice before everything else, and the rest will come to you as well. So do not be anxious about tomorrow. Tomorrow will look after itself."

As I drove back to the ranch in the darkness of the

desert, I could only envy those so-called poor people of Sasabe. Why did they have the luxury of their felt, lived acceptance? In the world that had raised me, such emotions would be considered embarrassing. You just didn't go around weeping and gnashing teeth, and certainly you couldn't accept the awful humbling of the supplicant: ask and you shall receive. To ask someone like me to be as the birds was idiocy. In my reality, there was no way I could respond to it. Christ had been talking to peasants who couldn't possibly have foreseen the complex challenges of the age in which I lived. Every iota of my training had told me to give up the child and the dark superstitions of blind faith. Technical progress had swept away such innocence. The problems of my world demanded that I or any rational man evolve into his own deity, controlling our lives by our own superior intellects.

How ludicrous, for example, were I to quote the parable of the birds to my banker when I didn't have enough cattle sales to pay off my debt. Or a corporate executive: could he convince his stockholders that he was going to keep increasing profits without storing anything in barns? What about controlling inflation, or staying even with the Soviets? Could we make that happen simply by letting tomorrow look after itself?

No, my training had led me to demand game plans, quotas, actions, results. Replace faith, hope, and charity with management, research, insurance.

And where had I come with it? I asked myself. To the stillness and simplicity I'd seen in the faces in the Sasabe church?

No, I was a long way from it. Those people could accept the existence of God and feel their primitive yearning for Him because they had interwoven it into their culture for so many centuries they couldn't possibly ignore it. They'd made it part of their scenery, like the rock creches with the dead flowers or the rude wooden cross that the wetback had placed on our Las Delicias mountaintop.

But my culture had suppressed the yearning, indeed had scientifically exorcised it out of me like a prehensile tail. Because spirit was an instinctual thing, being thwarted by modern rational society, my longing for spirit would simply have to surface somewhere else. This, of course, was what Solzhenitsyn had meant about dispersing spirit, rather than centering it on God where it belonged.

Well, I had surely learned to disperse mine, and the process had begun long before that night in Sasabe. In my "education," which the people of Sasabe had been spared, I'd spent years having experts teach me mathematics, dead languages, histories of cultures: probing everything except what I was inside. I'd received no instruction, no encouragement to address myself to the profound meaning of all life, and specifically my own. In my relentless education, I was never asked to question whether my spirit was important. In truth, the subject simply never came up.

If I must discuss it, let it out of the bag like a secret vice so to speak, the implication from my society was: put it in a plain brown wrapper. At a dinner or a bull session, talk about sports, politics, business, or war—but to touch on the idea of God, forget it, ruin a good party.

Yet if the yearning still persisted, boringly unanswered, then take it to a church, talk to another expert, a minister or priest. Well, I'd tried this too, but most of the priests I'd known had buried spirit far back in some musty theologic file. It was either too complex for me to understand, the way they presented it, or something of so little value it had been smothered in the spiritual rubber goods: the do's and don'ts of ethical living, collections, sodalities, pomp and penances; the rote of religious bureaucracy. Instead of journeying into my primitive longing, I found myself too often thrown into something that resembled a religious Lions Club or Rotary. My inarticulate spirit was hungry for the steak but ended up only with the sizzle.

So if I were not trained to fulfill the yearning by education or religion, I could hardly expect the cold commercial world of real-life to provide it. The heritage of my times had urged me to go out and thrive in society: the training for competition seemed vastly more important than any murking around in the swamps of metaphysics. If society didn't cherish it—there was obviously no dollar value on spirit—why should I? And so it became an irrelevancy, growing more and more remote from me until I couldn't feel it at all.

If it had to come out in me—and of course it did because it was my urge for completion, then I would be forced to *misdirect* my spiritual longing into one of the socially acceptable forms. Often, I'd hurl myself into excessive work, to seek my solace there. Or then an issue would come up, say an election campaign, and suddenly I'd make politics into spirit: the care and perfecting of man through man-made techniques. It seems the custom of our age to pursue this political spirit-substitute with such religious fervor that when one of our man-made gods topples, we go into a frenzy of desecration on his failed altar.

Even my much beloved Nature, and my struggles to protect it—here again, an obsession with this worthy goal often served as a spirit-substitute, one of the biblical false gods. I could see my worship of them along with most people's: the longing to lose ourselves in career, power, fame, money; to make jogging not an exercise but an adoration; to fling ourselves into self-fulfillment programs— physical, dietary, psychic, sexual—anything to give us transcendence. It wasn't the mere participation in these harmless and often beneficial pursuits that trapped us. It was simply our excessive hope in them, our deification of them, that they were the way to our completion.

No, as I thought that night, little wonder that there was not peace in me yet, and perhaps never. But all the way home in the dark desert, I did carry with me the stillness of those people of Sasabe.

The muted fervor of their faith, their certain knowing—that was their poorness, their humility that I yearned now to be mine. To give myself to God in the physical and emotional totality—yes, the child, the stricken, the powerless—to keep crying out again and again: God help me! Without You, I am only alone, Stay with me now and forever. Lead me . . .

Over the Christmas holidays, the boys all came home. Tom was working for a publishing house in New York, and with a determination I envied, was moonlighting his own first novel at night. John had just been accepted at the Harvard Institute of Design, where he'd begin his long road toward becoming an architect. When Peter arrived from Colorado College, it was like old times. Teddy and I delighted in our closeness. Though the double ranch life had been a bizarre and often taxing adventure, it had profited us richly in the rewards we'd had as a family. The boys were back out on cattle drives or breaking young horses, and when there was time left over, they had touch football games or made thundering night trips to Nogales to play guitars or stomp La Bamba in the discos across the border.

Rita was still taking care of Teddy and the household chores. She was clearly a conscientious, talented girl, and so with Christmas coming, we understood when she told us that she was going home. She came from a large family in Indiana, and after the holidays would return to college there. But in our family, any plan is subject to constant change. After we'd made a horseback trip up Chiltipiñes canyon to cut a juniper Christmas tree, Peter conned his brothers and Rita into a better idea. We'd all go to Mexico for Christmas, where a friend rented us his beach house at a shrimping town on the Gulf of California.

On the three-and-a-half-hour trip down, Tom and John rode with me, in a ranch truck creaking with mesquite firewood. Going down, we'd bring our landlord friend replacement fuel for winter, and coming back—Teddy's eyes gleamed: an empty truck! Into it we'd load a ton of Mexican cast-iron stoves, the pesky design of which hasn't changed for two hundred years. Because our old Las Delicias adobe had no central heat source, and often was so cold we'd have to cook breakfast with coats on, we'd now pepper the house with iron potbellies. Not your decorator's dream, but infinitely appealing to Teddy's Scarlett O'Hara frugality. And, because she was the ranch bookkeeper who had to pay the exorbitant electric heater bills, I had to go along with her.

(I had not foreseen at that point two givens of Mexican woodstoves: (1) somebody had to cut infinite amounts of tiny mesquite slabs to feed the damn things. If there was no wetback around to do it, and there usually wasn't, the job was mine all mine. Then came lighting the cussed monsters, which was an art that Mexican children apparently learned when they were big enough to toddle. But for the life of me, I have never been able to keep a woodstove going, and ahead lay long hours of breathing, fanning, and pure cursing into the smoky iron bowels. Yet let some Refugia or wizard Mexican girl come along with a ball of newspaper and a fistful of tiny sticks, she'd have a roaring fire in thirty seconds. Speaking of which hazard, (2) installation. Bartolomeo, our old deaf cowboy, was quite the ranch carpenter, so we gave him the stovepipe jobs up through the roof. By Christmas the following year, he'd managed to get the kitchen stove installed. Unfortunately, we'd just blown a lot of insulation material into the adobe attic, a commendable energy saver, but in the process ancient woodchips and detritus had been lodged against Bartolomeo's uninsulated stovepipe. On Christmas night, we returned from a party to find the kitchen filled with smoke. The attic was a surly, swirling inferno, crackling with burning electrical wires. Because the Las Delicias lay too far from civilization to be served by any fire department, we became it. For three days we were pumping hoses up into the attic until finally the roof plaster gave up the ghost and collapsed on our heads. Remedy: start all over again; put in a new kitchen, this time with an insulated stovepipe and, yes, a monstrous electric forced-air furnace, just to be on the safe, warm side!)

The beach in Mexico was wind-howled and freezing cold. We sat in the big Spanish house, huddled by the fire, and watched whitecaps spraying across the Sea of Cortez. It seemed, in fact, that the only people who went outside were Peter and Rita. They'd bundle up and run and play on the sand. On the way back to the ranch, Peter said unofficially that Rita was going to resume her college studies all right, only not back in Indiana. She'd decided to go to school in Colorado Springs, where Peter was.

A few eyebrows lifted. The baby of the family? It seemed pretty steady work, Pete and Reet. But those were the years when all of the young had soul relationships. Tom and John had been through theirs, and now Pete was entitled to his. The intensity of these affairs was something Teddy and I deplored, but we knew that in the drift of the country, the breaking down of the old ways, we couldn't do a damn thing about it. Besides, we had come to admire Rita greatly, and we'd miss her now.

After the boys had gone, and the Christmas tree been chopped into kindling for the woodstoves, there was a visible slump in Teddy. I told her that her exhaustion was obviously from the holidays, trying as she always does to make a celebration out of every family event. Then too, she was still taking the cortisone derivative for her liver, and though she showed great improvement, a certain amount of fatigue now seemed part of her life.

But other realities were closing in. For all our yearning to free ourselves to the spirit and get off the world, we still had anything but a simple lifestyle. I'd go to my desk each day and begin to write of the Pacific, but before long the telephone would ring or Bartolomeo would be rapping on my window. The San Miguel tank had gone dry. Start hauling water to keep the cattle alive. Then a pipeline would break or a new well had to be dug. But the tractor was shut down, needed a new transmission. Then in Wyoming, improvements in the hay meadow had to be made. Buy culverts, rent backhoes. Instead of paddling around a quiet reef at Pelelieu, I found myself floating on a stream of unpaid bills from both ranches, with a cow market that resembled the river Styx right then. According to the computers, we could look forward to at least three more bad years. All this and drought too. Something short of spec-tacular, as ex-podner would have said.

One night, after jiggering the numbers around for hours, I reached an obvious solution. Something had to go. We had to center ourselves somewhere. Initially, of course, we had hoped to accomplish this in Wyoming, but when the ranch proved too isolated for me, too unfeasible economically, we'd seized on Arizona as a place in the sun for a few months each winter. But by now, another truth had become apparent. As a neighbor put it: "Son, a desert ranch is a hole in the rocks to pour money in." Under Faustino's tenure of mismanagement, and the sketchy operation during the feedlot era, poor old Las Delicias was now beginning to crumble before our eyes. I'd learned that you can't run a ranch as a winter resort. Each piece of land requires year-round care and feeding. On the other hand, the Las Delicias, just by climate and proximity alone, did have more potential as an operating unit and lifestyle than Wyoming ever would.

Teddy was working on her own version of the ranch books when I walked over to her office and dropped a piece of paper in front of her. "The numbers will show you," I said. "We sell off the lower half of the Wyoming ranch, get rid of the houses, which are nothing but problems for you. By keeping the upper pastures, we'll be able to go up for a few weeks in the summer and get out of the desert heat. But the important thing, in this sale, we can clear all our debts, have some left over, and use that to fix up the Las Delicias and make it our one and only home."

At first, Teddy was stunned. Though we'd discussed such drastic action many times, the reality of it was like a death in the family. We weren't prepared. All Teddy could think of were the years she'd put into the Wyoming house, the hard-earned roots. "But you want to simplify," I kept telling her. "Something has to go."

"Darling, the boys love it so much, they'll never forgive us."

"Sure, they love it, but you do the upkeep. They'll get used to the idea someday."

"I hope," Teddy murmured. And soon she was brightening. "I do want so much to be just in one place."

"You're practically there," I said, and smiled. "I'll start on it tomorrow. After all, everybody keeps telling us how beautiful the Wyoming ranch is. Now let's see if somebody will put his money where his mouth is."

Within two months, somebody did.

4

Winter of the Moose

It was almost six years since we had driven up to Wyoming, to begin our dream there. Instead of May, it was March now; we had no Travelall loaded with possessions, but only a mundane Ford we'd rented at the Salt Lake Airport. We felt a joyous lightness, passing the Holy Cross Hospital that we had put behind us. As we lifted onto the Wasatch plateau in the dusk, Teddy was eagerly scribbling lists of furniture in the Wyoming houses. We seemed to have two of everything, but she was delighted to cope with that, bursting with ideas of how she'd rearrange the rooms in Arizona, and hang her ancestral portraits from Mississippi in such a way that we wouldn't offend John, whose prize-winning oil paintings from Stanford now occupied the places of honor. As she totted up the list, it became evident we'd need a warehouse for all our accumulations. I suggested that we dump as much as we could on the new buyers. Nothing of the kind, Teddy said. We'd strip the wetback rooms and the old adobe barns in Arizona and save every stick of furniture for the boys. They were going to be married soon.

"They are?"

"Of course! And I'll be so damn glad to have one life, one set of loyalties. I can't believe it's finally happening, can you?" She frowned. "But suppose they back out, the buyers? Could they?"

"Not a chance," I said. "They're hooked. They're pioneers, just as we were." Then we both laughed. It was dark now. We had turned north onto the great Wyoming desert, the emptiness. No tourists, no cars at this time of year. Just ourselves, and our headlights picking up quiet flakes of snow.

I hardly seemed to see them. Instead, I was remembering the first time I'd driven this road. Teddy and I were still living in California, and I'd been searching all the western states for a ranch. I received more mail from real estate brokers than I did monthly bills, if that were possible. I seemed to know every Friendly Ed and Flying Rancher Joe from Albuquerque to Butte. I pored over ranch maps and carrying capacities, and drove up hundreds of lonely roads. I advertised for what I wanted, resuscitated ancient friendships with people who lived in the West, and they'd write back and say, Yes, maybe neighbor Charlie or Widow Mock was thinking of selling, so I'd drive up Charlie's and Widow's roads too, arriving to find some forlorn kingdom with the fences broken, house sagging; no trout, no game, little grass; somebody else's dream, gone down. And even at that, they'd usually tell me, "We jist changed our minds about sellin' the home place." On one ranch, the "home adequate for ranching" turned out to be a railroad boxcar, abandoned by the Union Pacific when it laid the rails. Finally, in desperation, I'd taken to writing blind letters to chambers of commerce in obscure hamlets, to the effect: "California buyer [i.e., knowing nothing] desires to lay good hard cash on somebody with a beautiful little sportsman's ranch that can pay for itself." To my amazement, one chamber answered from the Wyoming mining town of Kemmerer. I snatched for my Rand McNally, located the place, and called the airlines. Teddy and I rushed up to find Kemmerer, surely one of God's most unlovely creations, set in coal spoil-banks, caving naked hills, and in that moment wind-wailed by a blizzard. We couldn't even get out of our motel until the next day. Well, we thought, the ranch was close and we could simply pop up there for a look. One hundred twenty miles later, counted in the pulse of the realtor's windshield wiper that never quite cleared the snow, we arrived in the Pinedale area. The name was encouraging, connoting trees somewhere, but they hadn't yet marched down to the mournful flat where we found, as the realtor's brochure put it, the "subject property." Subject, indeed! It was positively mendicant, huddling against snow-streaked buttes. "Now, that there cabin," the realtor said, pointing to a sagging eyeless hulk, "outlaws stayed there. Yessir, the Wild Bunch, Butch Cassidy and them, holed up here for winters." I could surely see why. "Good God," I'd said to Teddy, when we'd finally shucked off the realtor. "We could never live in a place as isolated as this!"

Three years later, we bought our ranch in exactly the same area, only more isolated. It must be something you have to work up to.

Now, as Kemmerer fell behind us, then LaBarge and the cut cliffs of the Green River where the immigrant wagons had crossed, I began to hope that my prospective buyers were of sturdier stock. One advantage they had over me in my first pioneering trip—they'd been frequent visitors to the Green River loneliness and loved to hunt and fish. My brother, Bill, who had put me in touch with them back in Chicago, said they were nice fellows, the very kind of people we'd want as neighbors. It was to be a partnership of these two gentlemen whose names, oddly, sounded like Hail and Farewell, so I simply called them that, to myself. They were certainly, as the ranch brokers say, qualified buyers, strong hands. And not only was there no ranch broker involved, thus saving us a commission, but Hail and Farewell seemed willing to pay us, for the lower half of the ranch and houses, five times what we paid for the entire ranch. I apologized for the asking price, but they were well aware of the appreciation, for they'd looked at quite a few other recreational properties. Once the deal was set, Teddy and I would simply move an old log cabin up to the beaver ponds and aspen on the remaining land. We would come and fish for a few weeks in the summer: virtually no upkeep, no headaches. Live happily ever after.

It was nearly midnight when Teddy and I turned up the familiar old Cora road. I had expected to hear the tires thrumming on the washboarded dirt. I should have known better. The road was snow-drifted: as I went whining and mushing up it, the car seemed to be entering a tunnel, single-laned by hard snowbanks that rose ten or twelve feet where they had been pushed up by the county plow. "Well, it's still the same, isn't it?" I said to Teddy. "Late March, and it's still the North Pole." We were laughing as I pointed out the spot by Black Butte where our friend had gotten his horsetrailer stuck, that first day we had all come up from California. Imagine me trying to push him out in loafers!

Ping!

"Ote," Teddy said. "What is that?"

"Damned if I know." A red dashboard light had popped on. When I got out and opened the hood, I was in snow up to my knees, great wet flakes swirling around, as if determined to prevent us from getting the last five miles to the ranch. I slammed down the hood and told Teddy: "We're running so deep in snow the damn fan has stopped working. Radiator is boiling over, but I think I can bull it in. Hold on, here we go."

Nowhere. Without chains . . . who in Hertz would have thought about chains in March? . . . the car kept squealing its rear end back and forth, unable to get started again. "You drive, I'll push," I said to Teddy, and I did, until we'd inched up a tiny hill and I leaped in. "Gotta have momentum," I cried, "really ram it or we'll never get through this snow."

A moment later, Teddy was laughing. "Oh, darling. Isn't that wonderful. Look! A cow. No, two of them."

In the swirl of the headlights, a cow moose and a yearling were walking slowly ahead of us, going the same way we were, because it was the only way. They couldn't possibly scale a ten-foot frozen snowbank and get out. What a lovely bit of local color! If Hail and Farewell could only have been with us, I could hear them saying: Okay, scratch off moose. Now what else can we see on our new ranch?

But to us they were a real problem. In the ping-ping-ping, the red dash light glaring and radiator steaming, I'd come up to within feet of the lumbering hindquarters of the two moose. I was trying to hold my precious momentum and they weren't budging an inch. Their stubby tails switched at me; once the cow turned and bared her teeth. I began blowing the horn, which, in the overloaded electrical system, was now down to a tinny wail. "You'll hit them," Teddy cried.

"Dammit, I've got to get past 'em or we're stuck!" More

horn, the engine groaning now, trying to quit, the moose flinging out their yellow legs in an angry trot. Teddy was still pleading for the moose, I telling her to shut up. The big cow made a leap up at the bank, clawed, slid back. Then, with a massive lunge, she spun around. I caught one glimpse of her red eyes. She was running now: she knew how to run when she wanted to. In a flying leap she slammed squarely up onto the hood of the car, colliding with the windshield in an enormous *whap* that sent me rocketing back in the seat.

We were stopped dead, Teddy and I speechless. There was moose hair on the windshield and she'd kicked out one of the lights. In a great clunking of limbs, the moose slithered off the hood, shook herself, and then, to my amazement, began scuffing up the snow with violent pawings, lowering her head so she could jump *through* the windshield this time. Furiously, I was grabbing the clutch lever, spinning us into reverse; we went squiggling back, somehow finding traction because it was downhill, the moose pursuing, getting ready for her next leap. I had to back up nearly a hundred yards. Then we had a stand-down of at least two minutes before she finally turned and trotted north again. We repushed ourselves and got started, but as soon as I'd inch within fifty feet of her, like a great black Moby Dick, she'd shake her crusted hair and whip around for another charge. I'd back up again and defuse her. It happened three times.

"I can't believe it," Teddy breathed. "I never thought a moose would jump a car."

"Of course they will, when they're mad enough. Maybe she's trying to tell us something."

Teddy frowned. "Like what?"

"That this is Wyoming, and you never know what to expect." I didn't say any more, because I didn't know myself. Only I did begin to wonder if that cow moose weren't some kind of an omen, a whack in our teeth coming up.

The snow stopped by the next morning, and the crisp winter sun beamed down on Hail and Farewell and their wives. Because of our rather dramatic arrival, we began telling them moose lore stories, and when we went out cross-country skiing with them, we followed herds of moose on the river. The wives began snapping pictures, and reminded Teddy to be sure to give them her moose-cooking recipe. As we sluffed our skis along the river, I was astounded to see how nature was now cooperating. The ice had even melted in certain pools, and Hail and Farewell were getting trout fever, wanting to know exactly which holes they should fish when the beautiful five river miles would be theirs. We trudged around the log barns, out into the gentle, drifted meadows. Each place seemed to have a story for us to tell: that old sagging chicken house had been a scene when the kids made a home movie; there was the badger hole where John took his awful spill; and on along that fence line, Tom had almost been struck by lightning. At night, with bourbons in our hands, we'd be up in the poolroom, the walls a psychedelic maze of colors where the kids' friends, the hay crews in the summers, had painted their names. Farewell's wife said, "I don't see how you could possibly leave all this. We feel terrible about it, really. It's your home. Are you positively sure?"

"It's said, of course," Teddy said. "But it would give us delight, too, to know that you and your kids can have the fun here that we did."

On the last morning, the men and I sat in my office. We went over the terms. There was a detail here and there, proof of easements, schedule of payments, possible delay until fall. Minor things, really. What counted was their intent and ours that we had a deal. I said we did, and, in fact, I planned to go east shortly on some book business. We suggested that I stop off in Chicago, and we'd close the paperwork there.

Then they were gone, whining away on our snow machines that would take them to their car, down the moose road, and eventually to the airport at Jackson. After they'd left, Teddy and I stood on the porch in the warming sun. "Let's go skiing," I said. "The way this snow is melting, there won't be much of it left."

"But we'll still be able to ski from our cabin on the upper place," Teddy said hopefully.

"Yeah. I guess we can. Of course, the cabin won't have any power in it, and will be practically impossible to get to in twelve feet of snow."

"It will be so snug and simple, though. All we'll need is a woodstove."

"Great. Bring one up from Mexico."

"All right," Teddy conceded, "I've got a better idea then. When the buyers aren't using our house in the winter, I'm sure they'll be delighted to rent it to us for a week or so."

"*Our* house?"

"Well, it really is, darling."

"No, dammit, it's not. Not when you sell it."

"I suppose it does change things," Teddy murmured. Then we went out and skied for several hours. At least a dozen moose were standing on the river, benignly peaceful and quite beautiful. They didn't have a charge left in them, now that the omen cow had done her work.

The morning we were leaving, the first goose came back to the meadows. I watched her for a long time, beating her way across the log cribs until finally she settled onto the same hay stack she always used. She'd brush off the snow and lay her eggs in a nest of hay bales. And maybe by the fall, when the young geese would be strong and airborne, the flock would light again in the last open water beside the point. Only now, it would be Hail and Farewell making the sneak in the snow. They didn't strike me as the kind of fellows who'd miss, the way I had.

"All right," I said to Teddy. "Let's go." We drove down the long road in silence. Sure. Put it behind us. Simplify, when you get to the middle of your lives. That was common sense, dollars and cents.

But can you put a price tag on a dream? The search, the effort to seize it, the fighting to make a place in a community; all the struggle to build a fence or break a horse or level willows into a new meadow: no, you don't ever sell those things. You have to cut them out of yourself like plunging a spade into the earth and slicing off roots of sod. I thought of my forebears in Ireland: "digging turf," they called it, spading their tiny squares of peat to burn in their fires. I wondered if my love of the land, its sense of preciousness, came from them, because they'd never owned any. My Aunt Nora had told me that her grandfather was a road-builder for Lord Luchan, which must have been back in the late 1700s. When I returned to County Mayo a century and a half later, and drove through the purpling moor known still as "Carney's Field," I asked an old Irishman for the name of the present owner. "Lord Luchan, sor, of course."

When Teddy and I returned to Arizona, the telephone began to ring: Tom from New York, Peter from Colorado, John from Cambridge. Earlier, we'd discussed with them our decision to sell the lower part of the place. They'd told us, well, go ahead, if we felt we had to. But now that it was happening, a hardening had set in. After all, they said quite logically, it was the one real home they had: the investment of many years and much happiness. Was it worth all that much, the money we'd get for it, the alleged "freedom"? While Teddy and I were trying to defend our complex reasoning, my younger brother, Peter, stepped into the discussion, long distance. Peter is a hard-rock geologist businessman. "You're damn fools," he said. "You talk about a good investment, how could you ever have a better one than that land up there? If you're short of cash, sell stocks or anything else, not land. And if Teddy is too worn out right now to handle the upkeep, then hire somebody for a couple of years and simply forget about it. We'll all pitch in, do what we can. In short, just hang tough until you're sure how Teddy's health is going to be. Things have a way of changing, you know. Once that place is gone, you'll never get it back."

I suppose that's what younger brothers are for. Peter's bluntness stung me, but not so much that I couldn't admit that he was right.

A few days later, en route to New York, Teddy and I did stop off in Chicago. When we met with Hail and Farewell, I said that I was truly sorry for getting their hopes up, but we just couldn't bring ourselves to sell. If there was ever a change, they'd be the first to know.

The laughed, and seemed quite relieved. Actually, they said, from the moment they'd left the ranch, they were convinced we'd never sell. They wouldn't either, if it were theirs. And so we parted as friends; nice fellows, Hail and Farewell: their understanding was much appreciated right then. I could hope that someday they'd find what they wanted because, certainly, they'd helped us find what we did. For it was clear now that our search for simplification, for stillness, was not as simple as we had thought. No exterior change would accomplish it. Only an inner one.

I felt a great sense of relief. Things were indeed looking up. We'd dropped the other shoe, and the echo was not all that terrifying. Teddy was phasing out of the drug; her liver biopsies were good and she seemed to grow stronger each day. Meanwhile, we made plans to simplify Wyoming. There'd be no more Red River herds marching north from Arizona. Instead, I leased the Wyoming grass to a young neighbor and his wife. They were not only good friends but excellent ranchers. For five years they would run their cattle on the place and do the haying. In addition, the U.S. Fish and Wildlife Service was off to an enthusiastic start on the Sonoran masked bobwhite program. Or, more accurately, it was a learning experience for their biologists and us. With high hopes and documentation, we had hidden our first cage of birds in the tall grass of one of the leased pastures. When we returned in a day or so to check on them, we found feathers and bones. A party of wetbacks had opened the cage and eaten the entire covey! Cost to the taxpayers about five hundred dollars per bird.

After that, the cages were plastered with grim federal warning signs in English and Spanish. I ran off hunters and shooed bobcats away. Because we were using pen-raised birds from the Fish and Wildlife Center at Patuxent River, Maryland, they were simply not wild enough to survive very long against our numerous ground and avian predators. The biologists began reindoctrinating the bobwhites with tape-recorded danger calls, synchronizing these to a captive eagle they would release; he would swoop over and we would watch in delight as the birds learned to scurry back into their safe box. A few bobwhite were even implanted with tiny solar powered transmitters, which would beep away as they traveled across the ranch. More than once I had to explain to some mystified Mexican cowboy that the fellow wandering around out there with the rabbit ear antenna on his back was simply "un biologico," listening to the birds. The cowboy would go away muttering: "Poco loco."

It started out to be a lovely morning in Manhattan, unseasonably warm and balmy. I hailed a cab at 98th Street and told the driver to go down Fifth Avenue. There was no need to hurry. I just wanted to enjoy the sights, and had plenty of time.

"Well, I don't," the driver snapped. He twisted to me and jabbed at a bandage plastered over the stubble of his cheek. "This what they give you for paying your income tax, I suppose?"

He jammed into gear and went swerving out into traffic. A portable radio was blaring on the seat beside him, and when we'd squeal to a stop at a light, he'd twitch there waiting, flicking the pages of his *Daily News*. Obviously, I'd drawn a sourball; nothing to do but ignore him, so I lay back in the warmth of the seat and watched the sunlight filtering through the big trees of Central Park. But the driver's voice kept rasping at me. Where was I from? I told him Wyoming, to keep it simple, and he snorted: "Green pastures, hah? Well, let me tell you something. They give me one ticket to get out of this stinkhole, I'd slick my ass getting out, I would. This supposed to be America, is it? Well, let 'em have it!"

He jammed down the accelerator, and for the next fifteen blocks delivered a sermon about how the junkies had ripped him off that morning, beat him up for the third time in a month. Now he had to go file a police report. "So what?" he sneered. "Think you gonna catch junkies when you got a million of 'em in the city, maybe two million, drawing welfare, getting their butts powdered in some hospital. Tell you what I'd do with the bastids. Line 'em up against a wall, machine gun 'em!" His hands flung up and went pup-pup-pupping across the windshield; get everybody who was in on the take: politicians, cops, bankers, landlords; crooked lousy country. Blow it away!

At 72d Street, the barrage had lifted long enough for me to tell him to pull over. When I gave him what I thought was an adequate tip to help with his problems, he flung it into a cigar box and was still cursing as he drove off.

I began to walk then, wishing I'd never taken that cab. There was no need to. I was only killing time before a luncheon with my agent and my former editor on *New*

Lease on Life. Because the meeting was so important to me, I was hoping to be relaxed for it.

Normally, I love walking the streets of New York. Many memories flood back. Teddy and I had courted here, and later, when I was working in the city, the kids had gone to their first nursery school, up near the park. But somehow, that morning, the old familiar joy wasn't there. I felt light-headed, a little short of breath. I was also amused, but puzzled, by an excess of saliva in my mouth. What will the parasympathetic nervous system think of next? I seemed to be like one of Pavlov's dogs, salivating at the sound of the food bell. Okay, I thought: chalk it up to the excitement of being back in the city, anticipating the meeting. Then too, we'd had a wild social schedule the last few days. Teddy's sister lived in New York, as did many of our friends, leading invariably to cocktail parties, rich dinners: overdrinking, excessive smoking; over-pushing. Yet the normal hangover reaction was dryness in the mouth, not this wet strange yearning, tasting something that wasn't there.

I wondered if I couldn't take the city anymore, the pace of being back in the Big Game?

Once before I'd had a similar sensation. From the peaceful snows of Wyoming, Teddy and I had flown east to go to a funeral, and arrived in New York just after the Kent State shootings and the invasion of Cambodia. We were stunned by the panic we found. Old friends, whom we deemed perfectly rational people, were now devouring every news broadcast as if their lives depended on it; they'd rush out for all the editions of the papers, which simply told the same story in different headlines. Hostesses who rarely watched television were interrupting dinner parties, and we'd all have to flock in and watch some commentator's update. Seasoned businessmen were saying in grim seriousness that the United States was through, finished. They were making plans to withdraw their money and invest it in Switzerland.

Teddy and I kept looking at each other. Was this *our* United States? The savage pessimism, the violence of emotion seemed blown far out of any proportion we'd known. It was only when we came back to Wyoming that a sense of peace returned. Cowboys were fixing fences and delivering calves. Far from abandoning ship, they were sloshing around in irrigation ditches, so that they'd have a hay crop for feed in the winter ahead. Mostly, they were too busy to listen to the news, as if they'd heard it all and it would go away. It always had.

But now, four years later, I was not so sure. Faces on the street were filming past me: taut, hurrying, preoccupied; even kids on skateboards cursed each other. A taxi squealed into an intersection, narrowly missing a pretty girl who was crossing. She thrust up her third finger and jabbed it repeatedly in front of the driver's face.

I thought: where am I? Yes, I've lived in cities much of my life, expect the bustle, often love the dog-eat-dog excitement of it. But this now seemed to be something else. Though the panic of the Kent State era was gone, in its place I could sense a hardening, almost as if it had become a condition, a permanent reflex of anger. In the crowding, rushing time-chase, people were quivering like wine glasses at shatter pitch, noise, words-words-words building into a crescendo of fear. I recalled what Alexander Pope had written: "They had no poet, and they died."

Were these our poets ... my hackie, or that girl with her finger stiffened in the air? Like the pool game a friend's children played in their Park Avenue apartment: "Screw Your Buddy," they called it. Were they all of us, now, writing our last stanza?

Even among our friends, the people who supposedly had everything, life seemed to be a relentless fury to seize experience, sensation: compartmentalize life by the clock, rush to this luncheon, make telephone calls to that charity, squeeze in twenty minutes at the Metropolitan exhibition, then rush again to the yoga lesson, to relax. And whether it was performance on Wall Street, the tennis court, or in someone's bed, it never seemed enough, anymore. Husbands and wives, on their separate chases, passed in airports. Valiums were on the bedside tables, and sleep was followed by that desperation to fill time. If you didn't, if you slowed just once, you might hear the terrifying void of self. In such a carnival of overstimulation, it was small wonder, I thought, that sex became so massively important. It seemed to be the only calming, personalizing force left to us.

I had to smile then, remembering an auburn-haired, willowy young woman I'd met on an earlier trip to New York. I happened to sit beside her at a dinner party. Teddy was tired, feigning the flu, and didn't come. The young woman seemed reserved at first; we made the usual small talk, but as we began to dance, she looked up at me in a rather curious, focused way and said: "You're Lincolnesque, aren't you?"

"Ah ... pardon me?"

"You remind me of Lincoln."

"Oh." I didn't know if that was good or bad, but it was certainly different! My usual dancing partners tend to lapse off into stoicism at best. But not this young lady. Based on her original diagnosis, she now began giving a physical exam to my bony hands, coupled with observations about my shambling, awkward tallness. I didn't know how a rail splitter was supposed to behave in such a circumstance. I wanted to laugh it off, to the effect that Abe and I were both from Illinois; maybe that was the connection she had in mind? Her only connection then was her body glued to mine, and her whisper: "I want to spend four hundred hours with you. When can we start? Tonight?"

When I got back to the apartment, Teddy was sitting in bed reading. I had to tell her, indeed put it up in lights!

Teddy began giggling: "Look at you, you're just one big pussycat grin!" And in the next breath: "Well, was she really attractive?"

Shrug. "I guess."

"Don't you I guess me!" Teddy howled. "She was, I know she was! How did you answer her?"

"I said I didn't know where I'd be for the next four hundred hours."

"Come on..."

For just that moment, I felt like Walter Mitty, walking seven feet tall. Finally it *had* to happen, didn't it? All the working fellows, every character in somebody else's novel had propositions thrown at them day and night, apparently. How come never me? Yes, never! No tight-fannied little stewardess, not even a sagging cocktail waitress. I felt destined to go through life like Mr. Before in a deodorant ad. Even the actresses in Hollywood were so chaste around me they always scurried off and sat clenched to their husbands. But now to have a beautiful woman, and a smart one too... yes, indeed, I'd take my moment in the sun. Because that was exactly all I was going to get out of it! I was terrified. But I did add, to Teddy, that the young lady had invited us to dinner the next night: said she wanted to get to know *us*. That is, if Teddy felt like it.

Teddy's answer was to leap out of bed and begin choosing which dress she'd wear. "Getting to know *us*, is she?" she mimed, and by the time the next evening rolled around, Teddy had pouffed her hair and spent twenty minutes putting on eyes, only to take it all off so she'd have the natural look. Surprisingly, the evening turned out to be very entertaining. The husband was a bright, attractive fellow, enrapturing Teddy with tales of his smuggling days in Hong Kong. When I wasn't eavesdropping their conversation, the girl was telling me about her youth in the ballet, at the same time managing to slip me little grips and slow glances, heading inevitably to dancing; me with her, the old Rail Splitter trying to shamble his way out of this one. "You were terrific," I told Teddy later. "You absolutely swamped her."

Now it was Teddy's turn to do the beaming. "I know I did. The poor thing. I guess she expected to find somebody in horn rims and Levi's. Well, that's the end of that."

So we could hope. But apparently, there were not too many Abes around right then. The more I'd tell the young lady I wasn't the slightest bit interested in physicals or history lessons, the more she'd create excuses so that our paths would have to cross. But Arizona is a long way from New York, and it took about a year before I sat beside the girl again, at a dinner given by mutual friends. In plain view of both her husband and Teddy, she whispered, "You missed your chance. What's the matter with you? Are you just going to sit out there in the desert writing one book and then another book? Is that all the excitement you want in your life?"

When I told her, Yup, it was pretty much what I had in mind, she simply shrugged, turned away, and, I hear, found someone else.

Sic transit Walter Mitty.

As I walked down Madison Avenue that morning, I thought I could understand the girl better. She was only playing the game as it was played here. She needed her release, like a morning's squeezed-in doubles game, and I, for a moment, was the ball. Any thought of feeling or sentiment didn't count. In fact, it never came up. There simply wasn't time.

Now, as I entered midtown, the crowds began tightening around me. I passed a store window with several television sets tuned to the competing channels. People were pausing on the street to catch the latest news, a babel of conflicting soundtracks echoing with combat film from Vietnam: a wound still bleeding in Technicolor. We were still there, weren't we? And still too in the ghettos, with the black faces protesting, rioting; but the channels were snapping to Washington now, some other hearing room, other committees, interrogating, searching, searing the power madness, the hypocrisy and shame of our newest whipping boy, Watergate. I felt for a moment as if that crowd were sweeping me into a public confessional, lashing us together in silent curses for our guilts, our failed gods.

I thrust away, not wanting to watch anymore. I'd heard it too much! I didn't want to feel that way, yet I couldn't help it. I couldn't escape these media tides. Even a man on a mountaintop takes with him his culture. Suddenly my unease of that morning, my childish Pavlovian reaction seemed to be linked to a mass nervousness and lack of hope. Our restless strivings for status and possessions— mine right with them—the chase that siphoned off so much of our energy was clearly not satisfying our deeper need for completion, for the not-by-bread-alone part of life. As the Dutch psychiatrist Van Der Berg put it: "Spirituality is living in God's creation, an awareness of one's link to the beyond. He who belongs to an inside eats, drinks, works differently." Events seemed dramatically to be proving that we would relearn to live for our spirits, or perish. If society were to be healed and returned to its center force—this unspoken longing in us for God—first each one of us had to be healed, recentered, for we were the sum of society's parts. Our dark night of the soul was here, and mine a tiny shadow among the rest.

That spring, we felt it was high time to go to Colorado and see Peter. We'd never visited his college, and Teddy seemed to have some instinct that this would be an opportune moment. "Anything wrong?" I asked. Teddy shook her head. It was simply that Pete was involved in a new photography exhibition at a student center. He was very proud of it, and after all, we'd often gone to Yale and Stanford for Tom's and John's various events. Now it was Pete's turn.

Also, Teddy added, her doctor in Salt Lake wanted to check her personally. We'd fly there first, and return to Arizona via Denver. I shrugged and said, fine.

"You probably ought to see the doctor yourself," she added.

"Me? Aw, come on."

"You ought to have a checkup once in a while. I don't like this silly thing you have, this salivating."

"Now listen, that's nothing. I'm probably smoking too many pipes."

"Then I hope he'll make you quit. Just talk to him. Please."

Well, we were deeply indebted to this man for his healing of Teddy's liver disease. But internists, I found, have a strange way of not talking. My faintest nod of submission to a physical exam was interpreted as grounds for a full-scale onslaught: I was piped and pumped and probed from all angles and orifices, and when the doctor came in and sat down with my scores, he shook his head and was grinning. "What in the world did you do?" he said. "Catch it from your crazy family?"

"Catch what?"

He took a quarter out of his pocket and tinked it on his desk. "You've got an ulcer that big, in your stomach."

"An ulcer? Now look, you pulled out somebody else's picture. I've never had an ulcer in my life!"

"You have now. And you're jolly well going to cure it. We don't like to see them, at your age, in this place."

"What's my age got to do with it?"

"They can be malignant."

I was astounded, terrified. All this and salivating too. I thought I was the ulcer expert in the family! I'd had years of Teddy's ulcers, then Tom's, and what's more, I could tell them exactly how to turn the damn things off. Tell everybody, write a book about it, only I couldn't tell myself.

When the doctor prescribed me some slowdown pills, the label on the bottle read: "Take as directed, for anxiety."

"Anxiety?" I said to Teddy. "Is that me?"

"It must have been."

"Well, the hell with that! This has got to end now, doesn't it?"

"You're the only one who can take it away." She smiled, a little sadly. "And where have we both heard that before?"

As we flew over the Rockies to see Peter, I stared down at the majestic peaks, the snows beginning to melt, spring coming. I felt a rising anger. Except for malaria from the Pacific and pneumonia that came out of it, I'd never been ill in my life. Nor did either of my parents or brothers and sister have ulcers. Why now? Was it a self-inflicted wound? I knew damn well it was, it had to be. Unless I could learn to accept the twists and turns on the road, the failures, they would inevitably begin to wreak their vengeance on my body. How many self-inflicted wounds had I seen in other peoples' lives, their inner gears locked for so long that finally they would shatter and fly off to lodge in wherever the body was weakest? Long ago, as a newspaper reporter, I had interviewed a doctor at the Mayo Clinic who told me he estimated at least fifty percent of all disease could be traced to unresolved conflicts in the psyche. I remembered an old wives' tale about ulcers: that they came in people who couldn't mourn properly, couldn't weep, as if, so the story went, tears were the healing force.

For several days, we wandered around Colorado Springs with Peter; we met his friends, saw his trophies; and of course, Rita, our loyal ex-summer girl, was still very much in evidence. She was taking extension courses and financing them by doing seamstress work for the local opera company. The laid-back college life seemed much to Peter's liking.

In the usual nonscheduling of events, we drifted down from the mountains early one afternoon and stopped at a remodeled railway station. "They've got good draft beer and pizza," Pete said. "Want some?"

Sure. Only everybody else, it seemed, had also flowed down to this junction point. We were finally wedged into a tiny table, Rita across from Teddy, and Pete facing me. I was talking about something as vital as the new cattle lease we'd made up in Wyoming when Pete interrupted casually. "Say, speaking of summer plans, who's going to be around in August? Any of the family?"

"I don't know. Somebody usually shows up. Why?"

Rita and Teddy were chattering on about how Rita repaired the opera singers' dresses. But for an instant I did catch Rita's eye. She too was obviously eavesdropping Pete, the way he shrugged and and said, "Well, August is when Reet and I are going to get married. Up there. You know . . . the upper place, by the beaver ponds?"

Speaking of ponds—well, no, I couldn't speak. All the excess moisture that used to go and feed the ulcer now seemed to spring to my eyes. And Teddy, Peter, and Rita were all laughing. "Damn you!" I cried, "Did you know?"

"Of course!" Teddy was beaming. "Rita told me the first night we were here. We just wanted to see how long it would take before you figured it out."

"Well, Pete," I fumbled, "it's great . . . I can't believe it . . . the baby, and he takes the first leap."

"Bye bye, baby," Peter grinned. "And just be glad, Big O, you didn't dump the Wyoming houses, because we've got a million people coming. Why, Reet's family alone and her relatives will be more than twenty . . ."

They were off and running then, Teddy and Rita jotting lists of the parties we'd have, and who'd sleep where. I was totally out of it, father of the groom, which was exactly how it should have been. Later, when we all walked together around the campus, Pete said, quite seriously now: "Yep, Reet's a pretty spicy little filly, a real mind of her own. She's a lot like Fred. Got the spirit, you know."

"Yeah," I said. "I know."

And that time, I didn't have to snuffle, pretending I had a cold. As the old wives say, let the tears come, and I don't suppose it matters if they're joy or mourning. Maybe a little bit of both heals best.

5

Summer of the Golden Trout

The healing, of course, takes years.

The waiting for the stillness. In the dying of the old, a new man was having to be born. And in a sense he was twins, because the healing of him must only be the joining of my old self to my new one. Blending the hopes, the dreams, the best flesh of both into the synthesis that was the present, past, and future, centered now as one.

It was like watching a film spool backward in time. I wanted to say: but this is where I came in! Yet I was coming in now in a new way, in every place and experience.

At the same beaver ponds where only yesterday, it seemed, my old friend had caught his trophy trout, with the sadness in his restless smile—here in August, under the aspen, Peter and Rita were married.

Hardly had the honeymoon ended—they had spent it camping up at a mountain lake—when Peter informed me that he and Reet were enrolling in agriculture school at the University of Arizona. Little by little, with our agreement, Peter wanted to begin operating the Las Delicias. "Big O," he said, "you've really got more than enough on your hands with your writing. That's where your heart is. But mine's in the ranches, and so is Reet's. We want to make it our life."

And eventually they did.

So did John become an architect. In the process, he fell in love with his classmate at Harvard, Nancy Murdock, not only a charming girl and talented architect, but a Princeton graduate to boot! After three sons who wouldn't go near the place, I finally had someone to share my *Alumni Weekly* with, and, I hoped, a great deal more.

And so, too, did Tom set his life direction when his first novel was published, followed by articles, screenplays, and more books down the road. I found myself meeting with literary folk in New York and being introduced as: "This is the writer, Tom Carney's—[father]." And when Tom finally married an eminent photo-journalist, whose byline was often on the covers of newsmagazines or on billboards of new motion pictures, I was introduced as "the [father-in-law] of Maureen Lambray."

Clearly it was a time for second billings, and Teddy and I were proud of it. Not only were we entering the delightful autumnal role of being grandparents, but in the transition of watching our children replace us in their own careers, we were beginning to see our life in a different light. When the boys and their wives came home to the ranches now—Tom from New York, John from

Chicago—they would momentarily plug us into their frenetic urban existence. Even Peter and Rita's friends were mainly involved in the exciting growth of the Southwest. When John and Nancy would bring home plans in Arabic for a multi-million-dollar city they were designing in Saudi Arabia—when Tom and Maureen were hatching plots with a magazine to be smuggled into Afghanistan, dressed as tribesmen—their new world seemed light years away from Teddy milking her cow or me riding a horse up a desert canyon.

On a morning shortly after Peter had taken over the operation of the Las Delicias, he and I set out to cull our string of horses: decide which old ones had to be sold, and which colts warranted further breaking. As we rattled down out of the rocks of Chiltipiñes canyon, the herd came kicking and bucking ahead of us into the corral. They were all fat and sassy on the first green feed of spring.

All except Cora. She was a beautiful bay filly, a thoroughbred with four Kentucky Derby winners in her pedigree. Now, my love affair with thoroughbred horses went back a long way. When I was in my late teens in Illinois, I'd bought two old broken-down thoroughbreds that had limped off the racetrack. I'd paid four hundred dollars for the pair—and that was probably exorbitant! Nonetheless, I hung in with them and raised two colts which I was just starting to break when the war came. To my amazement, the colts made their way to a racetrack— by then I was so jungle-bound on the islands I couldn't believe people were racing anywhere in the world. But sure enough, at some mail call at Guam or Pelelieu, I'd received a soggy envelope with a breeder's check enclosed, ten percent of my colt's winnings.

So, having been bitten by the bug, I couldn't resist

when a friend offered me a thoroughbred race mare with weaning filly at side. Second childhood sort of thing, or the daughter I'd never had, and little Cora became it. I'd named her for our Population 3 post-office town in Wyoming, and her brother for Sasabe, Pop. 15. Some of my desert neighbors ran a few cheap, rocky-legged racehorses, and seemed to enjoy it a great deal more than the cow business. Anyhow, because cows were such a mournful asset right at that point, I began building my hopes for Cora to "win one for the Gipper."

But when she was a yearling and I was gentling her daily in the Chiltipiñes corral, she stepped on a nail or old piece of junk, and it created an abscess in her hoof. During the two years that the vet and I doctored her, Cora never again took a sound step. She was actually not walking on her damaged hoof but on the coffin bone within it. Thus, when she stood now in the corral with her head low and her eyes dull in pain, I turned to Peter and said: "That's it. I can't watch her like this anymore. Ship her to the auction on Friday."

Dog meat. Well, it almost broke my heart. I went back up to my adobe office and tried to bury myself in the typewriter. Soon, on the warm spring breeze, I heard a metallic tapping. Out of curiosity, I followed it to the corral, where I found Pete putting a set of shoes on Cora, shoes that would lift the coffin bone off the ground. "Are you crazy?" I said. "I told you to ship her."

Pete grinned at me with the horseshoe nails still in his mouth. "Aw, hell, Big O. Give her one more chance. Take her up in the rocks of Diablo Canyon. If she can't cut it, then all right, blow her away."

She hadn't been ridden for nearly a year, so it was with some reluctance that I finally swung up and mounted. But she only stood like a whipped dog, and when she took the first step on shoes she shouldn't have been wearing, a rack of pain shivered up through her shoulders. I doubted if she could even walk the half mile over to Diablo Canyon.

In fact, she almost didn't. She stumbled and tried to fall several times. But in my desperation to save her life, I kept urging her. The Mexicans called this canyon Diablo for good reason, because it had sheer rock walls and a tortuous maze of steep arroyos. From a thicket of catclaw, a covey of quail exploded, gray in the sun. Cora didn't even see them. She had enough to do just to walk. "Poor Cora," I said, and touched her neck. Then I realized how ridiculous this was, and in pity began to turn her toward home and call it quits.

But her ears had trembled. For the first time her head moved, upward. A whitetail buck deer went bounding out of the rocks above us, his heels clicking in stiff-legged leaps. I noticed that Cora was watching the deer, and that she'd also begun to sweat. So I simply rested her there, both of us perching on the mountainside as we watched the deer springing all the way up to the rim of the canyon and over the top.

I don't know what happened in that moment. Cora cast a slow, puzzled glance down the steep trail, as if wondering how she'd ever got here. Was this really Cora? I remembered then that she'd never been able to follow the other ranch horses up into the rocks, because her feet were too tender. But now, her body gave a tremble. She tugged at the bit. "All right," I said. "You want to follow the deer?"

She gave a scramble, then a leap. Rocks loosened under her feet and she clawed at them, clumsy at first, but slowly we were inching up until she'd scrambled onto a small mesa. Softer dirt and less rock were here. "All right," I said again. "You can walk a little, can't you? Can you trot?"

I slid up the reins and didn't even have to touch her with my heels. She began to trot, flinging her hooves out, glinting in the sun. In my early attempts at training her, I'd worked her on a lunge line, in circles, and a professional trainer had figure-eighted her before her foot broke down. So now I shifted my weight and began cantering her in slow circles. She never missed a step. Then I'd slide my legs on her flanks and she'd change her leads. Unable to believe it, I scurried her down off the mesa until we reached a soft sand trail in the bottom of the canyon. Here, I gave her her head, and she began galloping in a smoothing thunder, running for the roses for which she'd been bred. When I finally pulled her in, perhaps a little hard, she snatched at the bit, her nostrils flaring red, as if she were saying, I know what you want from me. Just give me a chance to deliver it!

When we'd run all we could, I sat there on her, breathing hard, and with tears in my eyes. Because it was obvious that this little cripple, this neurotic reject all her life, had just realized that she wasn't. In those moments in Diablo, she had become somebody. She had found her sense of worth.

About that time, my next project came into being, and, ironically, it too was named after a horse. Through an odd combination of circumstance, I'd been hired by a major studio to write a film on the great Sioux leader Crazy Horse.

In typical Hollywood hyperbole, the studio people were crowing that this could be the definitive Indian story; that is, if the writer didn't blow it. In truth, Crazy Horse's actual story was so powerful that no writer was needed to tell it. All we would need do was open the history books, and hope that we could dramatize the man as the remarkable figure he was.

On the assignment, Teddy and I traveled through northeastern Wyoming, Montana, and South Dakota. We were retracing the fated steps of Crazy Horse in that summer of 1876 when, at the Rosebud and the Little

Bighorn, he defeated in one week the finest calvary troops in the world. And the secret of his victory was that he had conquered his worldly desires. He wanted no plunder, no fame, no power. He had filled his void with a spiritual belief so total, so accepting that he was prepared to die for it.

In interviews with Sioux in South Dakota, Crazy Horse's direct descendants—driving with them in a pickup across the tawny hills, or sitting in one of their darkened houses at dusk—I felt that spirit of Crazy Horse come alive. For good reason had he been called the Strange One by his people. Even in his boyhood he'd had supernatural experience, hardening his belief that man, animals, and earth were all one, centered in their God. As he'd cried later: "No man can sell the earth on which the people walk."

But the corrupt ones, the pharisees of his Siouan people, were indeed being driven to sell their vast lands. When Crazy Horse began to do battle against the encroaching whites, he showed absolute disdain for death. He was convinced that God had intended no bullet ever to kill him. In his repeated prayers, and fastings, he received vision after vision, describing to him in advance exactly where his enemies would be. As one of the present Sioux leaders, a relative of Crazy Horse, told me: "We know he had this power, but, of couse, what an Indian knows and believes, living out here, is almost impossible for a white man to accept."

No, I couldn't accept it at first. Yet as I dug deeper into obscure historical accounts and survivor reports, written by U.S. troopers and officers, the fact seems inescapable. Crazy Horse always did arrive when the U.S. forces least expected him. He appeared at the Rosebud when General Crook's men were breakfasting along the creek. They'd thought he was thirty miles away. He appeared at the Little Bighorn, *behind* Custer's defense position, and a good one it was—because, according to the Sioux, he had a vision of a coulee unseen to Custer. By leading a thousand Sioux and Cheyenne up this slash in the hills, he accomplished his terrible slaughter in less than fifteen minutes.

In later months, when a vengeful United States turned its entire frontier army against him, Crazy Horse, alone of the Sioux leaders, kept fighting on for his land and his God. All around him, the pharisees of his own people had surrendered or sold out. And when at length, Crazy Horse rode into Fort Robinson, Nebraska, to surrender the remnants of his starving band, one trooper witness said, "Hell, this ain't no surrender. It's their victory celebration."

But, of course, there could be no victory. A single believing, uncompromising man could not long stand against the worldly forces then assembled against him. No more than Christ could. So Crazy Horse became in those last months the Christ-figure of the Indian movement, an image that endures to this day. In a final Judas-kiss, one of his disciples killed him in cold blood, and not with a bullet at all, but a knife. Crazy Horse had foreseen even this, in a vision that showed blood running down into his moccasins. As a mourning Sioux said, when they pulled an army blanket over Crazy Horse, with the U.S. insignia across his face: "He has wanted death. Now it has come."

The dream I saw in Crazy Horse fired my admiration for the man—a man who had filled his void with something greater than himself. His struggle had become mine.

Yet when I returned to Hollywood with my screenplay hot in my hand, a studio executive snarled: "What in hell are all these Indians doing in this picture?"

"But it's *their* story."

"Who gives a damn! They all look alike. Dumb faces and too confusing. Besides, we can't get an eight-million-dollar budget on some no-name Indian actor, Joe Eagle-Feather; forget it. Put white people in it, so we can attract a strong lead, a star who's bankable. And besides, these Sioux have the reputation of being hard to work with, they gouge you."

"But Crazy Horse is the Sioux Christ figure."

"Forget the Sioux. We'll shoot it up in Canada where we've got some trained movie Indians, cheap. Or, use Mexicans."

All right, all right, the studio executives finally said, there's something in the story, sure, but it plays too downbeat, the guy dying in the end. Who needs it? And what about the cost of all this Indian makeup? By now the budgets had come in. "But the Sioux," I kept saying, "want to do the movie, and they'll even provide their own buckskin and beadwork."

Crummy stuff. The budget says it will cost a hundred sixty thousand dollars just to wardrobe and coiffure Crazy Horse's wife. The broad is only in the picture for two scenes. And that Little Bighorn battle—we've seen it a thousand times. It'll cost a million bucks now. Drop it.

Also drop the snow scenes. "But you can't," I said. "The only way the army destroyed Crazy Horse was to run him down in the winter."

"Then make it a light winter. Better, Mexico."

And now enters a director, a "name" whom the studio would finance. His suggestion: "You've got too much of this smoky teepee routine, this spiritual stuff. So in one of these teepee sequences we put a sex orgy; that's right, naked bucks and squaws having at it so they'll come alive. Also, Crazy Horse's father...you play him just as this stodgy old medicine man...well, show him *with it*. Human desires. We put him out there in front of the teepee, under a blanket with Crazy Horse's mother. No big sex, just kind of working her over, and they're both laughing about it. Loving it."

Human desires.

Well, they don't die easily. In fact, it took me seven years of writing and rewriting Crazy Horse before the consensus seemed to emerge that it was not commercial, this spirit thing. Nobody would gamble on it. "Blacks, yes. Do something on them, take a *Roots*, they're a power bloc, they spend money, buy tickets and T-shirts and teddy bears. But Indians, hell, there aren't enough of them to count, and who cares anyway?"

Well, obviously I'd cared, and was still waiting for the telephone to ring with good news on Crazy Horse when another old horse showed me how little it all mattered.

It was our spring cattle drive, beginning in the dark cold of 4 A.M. when I walked into the adobe barn and hollered for Red. What answered was a snort, then hooves rattling as Red escaped into the corral where he hoped I couldn't catch him. The arch, proud way he tossed his head seemed to be saying: I *am* somebody—and, in truth, Red was.

Back in his long career, I suspect, he'd been on the racetrack. He had the hauteur of having run for the roses. Later, he became a high-goal polo pony, summering on Long Island and wintering in Florida. His picture appeared in *Town and Country* as he stood between pretty women who were petting his nose and pouring champagne into the silver trophy he'd won. After such a life of glory, it was understandable that Red resented spending his autumn years on a dusty, forgotten Arizona ranch.

Also, like his master, he didn't like getting up early to work. When I had the indignity to bridle him, he tried to pull away. I ignored that, but then as I tightened the cinch, he jumped right out of the saddle. "You restless sonofabitch," I said, and kneed him in the ribs. "Now look..." I grabbed the headstall of his bridle..."you may not like this any better than I do, but we're going to do it, understand?''

On such a brave oath, I cinched him, and we rode off to follow Teddy, Peter, pregnant Rita, and a pair of cattle dogs. Now, it would take quite a dour fellow indeed not to be enthralled by the sunrise on the desert. My problem, and I think Red's too, was simply a matter of priorities. His desire was clearly to be back in the barn eating, or flirting with the mares. To be forced to thunder across a rocky desert for hours, pursuing dumpy, smelly, always stupid cows was definitely not what Red had in mind for a retirement home.

In my case, the longer I was out on roundups, the more time I'd be away from the vigil at my desk, in case "they" called about *Crazy Horse*. To expect our terrified little Mexican girl of the moment to answer it was not to know the wetback culture. Only if the studio operator persisted, because Hollywood always rings twice when it thinks it needs you, might the little girl timidly snatch up the receiver and blurt, "No sabe. Señor no esta aqui," and slam it down, squarely on my future. Therefore, with all this dizzying potential awaiting at *my* feed trough, what the devil was I doing galloping an old horse back and forth across a wasteland of mesquite?

Like the cold rainy day in Wyoming, with Rex at the bridge, I had an instinct we were heading for a crash. After an hour or so of riding in the dawn, and locating few cattle, Peter decided to change tactics. He came rattling down in our truck and trailer and hauled us eight miles to the north end of the ranch. Here, as the sun rose, we'd begin sweeping from north to south, instead of vice versa.

Teddy and Rita spurred off happily in the new game plan. We couldn't ride enough hours to satisfy them. But the more I wanted to hurry and get home, the slower the roundup proceeded. Somebody missed a bunch of cows hiding in an arroyo. I charged back and forth, chowsing a bull several miles to the corrals, only to have Pete explode at me: "Dammit, Big O, couldn't you see he was crippled? I told you to leave him where he was."

After five hours on the trail, we'd gotten no further than the first big corrals. Now, coughing in the dust, we began the lugubrious job of sorting and counting the milling herd. The sun seared up to high noon. There was no lunch, only Granola bars and a couple of squashed peanut butter sandwiches, which I detest. But we were short-handed, and cattle don't move well in the heat, so we had to keep them going.

Our eventual destination was the headquarters corrals, four miles away, our tiny white adobe shimmering like a mirage against the mountains as we inched toward it. At this point, a young friend of Pete's cantered up to help us. He was a good kid, a good roper. In fact, to demonstrate his skills, he threw his loop over a big calf in the midst of the herd. The calf gave a buck and bawl, and jerked the rope out of the boy's hand. Now we had panic, the calf charging wildly back and forth through the cows, which were beginning to break and scatter all over the desert. "Big O!" Peter shouted. "You and Rita hold the herd!" An eight-months-pregnant girl and an old man on an old horse trying to surround six hundred hot, cranky beasts. Great. As Rita and I began "whoaing" and blocking, Pete and the youthful roper thundered after the wild calf, which was now being pursued by its enraged thousand-pound mother. Pete had his rope whipping over his head, then, a spray of sand in the sun, his horse went floundering into the tunneled earth of a pack-rat warren. Why he didn't cartwheel I'll never know; one usually does, striking such terrain on a dead run. But finally Pete did manage to get a rope on the calf. He was about a half mile from me, holding the calf, when Teddy came to his assistance. She dismounted and began to pull the first rope from the squalling calf's neck.

With Red champing and sweating, I heard myself screaming: "Look out!" But Teddy was too far to hear me, nor did she see the enraged mother cow racing down on her. At the last moment she turned. What I saw was the awful slow motion that films like *Crazy Horse* use when they don't want you to miss the blood and gore. The cow butted Teddy square in the stomach. A tiny doll-like figure hurtled upward end over end and fell limp into the sand.

Red never covered a polo field so fast. By the time I pulled up next to Teddy, she was grinning and brushing herself off, with the little cattle dogs yapping and holding the cow at bay. "My!" Teddy said. "Isn't she a conscientious mother!" Pete was grinning too, telling me to forget about it. Everybody was all right.

But still the calf had the first rope on his neck. "Dammit," I said, "you've made a mess of this. Now I'll get that thing off." I reached down from Red, grabbed the rope and began tugging it loose from the calf's head. But the dogs couldn't hold the cow. She came smacking into Red's shoulder, ramming him again and again. Bless him, he managed to keep his footing. Indeed, he was so humiliated to be treated like a common cowpony, he bit the cow.

But what nobody had taught Red on the polo fields of greener pastures was that you don't step into the loop of a rope. Don't ask me how the new rope got on the ground; there were many ropes out. This one was connected to something, so that when Red stepped into it, the loop went tight on his ankle. He reared up to go over backward. I scrambled off him just in time to see the cow bearing down on me like a black locomotive six feet away. As I pedaled backward desperately, I tripped and fell, spread-eagled, my soft underbelly cringing before her giant hooves.

At the last moment, a cattle dog bit her on the heel. She

turned and I scrambled away to hide behind Red, who had now stepped out of the rope. Laurel and Hardy on the range. Well, finally it was all over and everybody was laughing, particularly Pete. "Look, Big O," he said, "you didn't want to be out here today anyway. Now that we've got the real work done, we can take 'em the rest of the way. Why don't you just load Red into the trailer and go home?"

I felt like breathing: I thought you'd never ask! But cliché or not, it was the only idea around, and I seized it. Remounting Red, I loped him off across the wasteland of the north pasture, where this fiasco had begun so long before it seemed like last week.

By the time we reached the truck and trailer, Red was lathered black, the veins standing out on his legs, and his head lowered between them. As I put him into the trailer, I patted him and said, "Don't worry, oldtimer. We're almost home now." Red could feed his ego at his trough and flirt with the mares, and I could be poised at my desk awaiting my telephoned manna from Hollywood.

Then I got into the pickup and turned the key.

Key?

No, it wasn't in the ignition. It also wasn't under the seat, or in any of the devious places Pete chooses for it. The key was simply in his pocket, so far from me now that I could barely see the dust of the moving herd.

They would be home long before the old restless rushers, Red and me. The look Red gave me when I took him out of the trailer and mounted him again was only indescribable abandonment. If horses could have cried, the pair of us would have done it together. He was so tired, so disgusted with all the needless outrage of this day he could barely walk. And thus we began sluffing the last seven miles home. When it became obvious that Red had reached what the racehorse men call his "bottom," I got off him and we both walked.

Probably it was the one wise thing I did all day. Because, about three miles after we'd set out on our death march, we came to a barbed-wire gate. As I pulled it open, there was a rattling beneath my feet. Red recoiled, his nostrils flaring. In the debris by the gate, I saw the telltale glitter of bars and stripes: a diamondback rattler.

But then I was laughing, kicking the damn thing. It was no more than a dry skin that a rattler had shed however long before. And the "rattling" sound, so apparently synchronized to it, was my boot, crackling into the dry pods of a locoweed.

Perhaps it was hunger or fatigue, but I felt a sudden liberation, as if that snakeskin were some big baggage I'd just discarded myself.

Suppose I could see every moment—even a few of my moments . . . with the clarity of fright, the sensation of that threatening snake? Suppose I could enjoy just the here and now of it, and being what I now was? Not a somebody, just me, doing nothing important for the State of the World except taking a spectacular ride in God's country. And instead of restlessly wanting to be somewhere else— loving this, cherishing these blessed instants. Because what else did matter?

So, yes, "we" laughed. Red and I. I didn't know what time we finally got home. Anyhow, for all our impatience, nobody seemed to miss us. In fact, they never even called.

Through the strapping lady archaeologists who were still digging for Indian artifacts on the ranch, I had occasion to meet the "Bone Man." He was a forensic pathologist at the University of Arizona, a fascinating fellow who helped the girls identify and date any questionable materials they'd uncovered. As we rummaged around his laboratory, he showed me box after box of musty femurs, tibiae, finger bones, and skulls sent to him by police departments across the country. His job was to describe the victims of these disappearances or foul play and estimate their sex and age. When he learned that I lived on a ranch in the Altar Valley, his eyes gleamed. "Why, do you realize," he exclaimed, "that valley is one of our most active areas. Right now, I must have at least five or six fresh skulls that have been brought in from there. Would you like to take a look?"

I wanted to say, if you've seen one, you've seen 'em all, but he insisted, and began pulling out neatly tagged craniums. "Caucasian male, I'd say about twenty-five, three bullet holes, small caliber...Mexican or Indian female, age indeterminate, death from some sharp object..."

"But all these bodies out there...who did it, why?"

"That's the police's problem, not mine. Some of them are obviously wetbacks, maybe a few runaways thrown in. And many have to be drug-related murders. After all," he smiled, "that's a big, lonely valley. Good place to lose somebody in."

Good place indeed! The Las Delicias, though nineteen square miles in size, was a peanut compared to our neighboring ranches. Some encompassed a hundred square miles, nothing out there, no houses, roads or lights—only a dark sweep of mesquite, cut by rock arroyos where there were lion tracks in the sand, and coyotes howling perhaps just to hear their own voices.

Late one night, not long after I'd talked to the gleeful pathologist, I was just going to bed when I realized I had forgotten to get the mail that day. I happened to be alone in the house. Teddy was in Chicago, visiting John and Nancy. Now, because mail for me happens to be a ritual contact with the outside world, going to bed without it is like not brushing your teeth. I got into the truck and drove down the four miles to the mail box. After I'd collected what few bills there were, and yesterday's paper,

I made a U-turn onto the Sasabe road and started back up to the ranch house. I'd gone a mile or so when I happened to glance in the mirror.

Lights were following me, and they were coming fast. Well, I thought, who?—and began ticking off the various possibilities. It couldn't be the only other person on the ranch, deaf old Bartolomeo, because he lived five miles away and was always asleep with his chickens. Furthermore, he didn't have a car. He rode a horse when he wanted to come up and see me.

Perhaps a lost deer or javelina hunter? Well, no, it wasn't hunting season—and it damn well wasn't the meter reader, particularly because the lights were gaining on me, eating up my dust. What about neighbors? I asked myself hopefully. Some emergency? But it would have to be a helluvan emergency for one of these rough desert types to make a sixteen-mile round trip to see me— particularly when they knew that if, say, their water line had blown, I was the last fellow in the world who knew how to fix it.

By this time, I had sped up myself, swerving into the last arroyo from which I could see the dull white outline of the house. For some reason, not clearly thought through, I figured if I could get into the house—then what? No way to barricade the ninety-year-old adobe. Even tiny birds managed to penetrate whenever they wanted. But of course I had my quail guns and the quick-grabbed phone to the sheriff.

Ah, the hell with it, I thought, and by now, any worry had been replaced by just plain anger at whoever this clown was who had tailgated me through four miles of my own turf. I banged open the door and got out.

A few yards behind me, the engine running, stood a black car, distinguished only by the fact that its fenders had been abused. It had no license plate that I could see, and when I'd moved out of the glare of the headlights, I found myself looking at a stripped-down wreck that befitted the man who came toward me.

He was a tough punk with a swarthy face, sideburns, unkempt hair, and a black leather jacket. "All right," he said, "who are you?"

"You mean, who the hell are you, driving in here, following me?"

"Was that you, made a turn out on the road?"

"Damn right it was! And why shouldn't I? This is my ranch, and I was going down to get my mail!"

"Your ranch, huh?" His right hand was moving toward his belt.

"Yes, And you can jolly well back that car out and get off it!"

His eyes glimmered in the light, half a smirk and half a go-to-hell. Then he jerked a black object out of his pocket. I can't say I almost grabbed for it. A quicker man might have. But when his hand moved toward the light I saw a wallet and a card of some sort in it. "Treasury Department," he said. "Undercover."

I was so relieved I almost asked him to spend the night! But then again, on a closer look, no. He wasn't a public-relations-type cop, not this bird. I later met others like him in a story I was doing on drugs. These were the front-line troopers, mostly surly, twitchy scarfaces, all young, because none of them lasted at it too long. Not sitting out there in lonely cars in the Altar Valleys of the West, waiting to make a heroin buy from men who came by car or horse or plane, professional killers who had the latest automatic weapons in their laps in case the "buyer" didn't smell right. And even if he did, after the money had changed hands, they would often blast him away anyway, so they could sell the goods over again.

One agent I knew had walked into a Mexican hacienda to make a heroin purchase. When the deal went wrong, the mobsters opened up with a .50-caliber U.S. machine gun, complete with tripod. The agent came to in a Mexican hospital, his chest split open and flies crawling in the wound.

As for my visitor, standing there in the darkness, all he'd say was that he was waiting for a car that would be coming east from the mountains. "We had a buy set up with some people," he said. "I saw your lights make that turn; I figured it was them and they were splittin'. Excuse it, huh? I gotta get back out there."

"Yeah," I breathed. "I guess you do."

When he drove off down the road, he didn't use his lights. Once in a while I'd see him punch his brake at an arroyo and the red would flash. Then finally the mesquite swallowed it up, and he went off to wait, wherever he waited, whatever for.

Alone. Both of us.

Maybe it's like the old story about the Lone Ranger and Tonto. When a thousand howling Indians surround them, Tonto looks at the Lone Ranger and says: "What do you mean, 'we,' white man?"

Well, "we" now was ourselves. That's what the new life demanded: an acceptance that we were out there pretty much by ourselves. Over the years on the ranches, I'd seen trouble hit from the most undreamed-of directions. Because there was nobody to help me, I had to help myself, with as much coolness and old lore as I could muster. And, after it was over and I'd shivered it all out, I longed to be able to laugh at the near miss. To do that would mean a letting go, a thankful admission that there but for the grace of God went I.

The bolt of lightning that today blew a five-foot hole out in our sagebrush—yesterday it caught a rancher friend who'd ridden in thunderstorms all his life. Act of God, surely, and no different from an automobile careening into you on some freeway. Yet out here the violence seemed somehow always lonelier, and more personalized.

Up in Wyoming, a young cowboy kid had ridden into the swirling Green River. He'd done it many times before, following his boss when they were moving cows out to spring pasture. But this time, something caused the kid to become separated from his horse. His horse kicked him in the head. A day later his brother came to me and asked to borrow my metal detector. The kid was wearing his rodeo belt buckle. They were trying to locate it on his body, somewhere downstream.

Or, there was a day during the fall hunting season when one of my brothers came down with a severe flu after camping out in a snowstorm. I drove him thirty miles to our closest doctor. When he entered the small shacklike building that served as the clinic, a young man in hunting clothes was lying on the sofa in the waiting room, the doctor standing over him.

"Oh, I'm sorry, Doc," I said. "Didn't know you had a patient. We'll wait outside."

"Come right in," he answered. "This one's dead."

A young, strong kid who'd hunted elk all his life. But this particular day when he'd downed his bull and was cutting through the brisket to dress him out, his knife slipped, plunged into the main artery in his leg. He was alone, fifty miles from town, and up in the high timber. Now what? Apparently he'd been cool enough. He pulled off his bootlace and made a tourniquet around his leg. His only mistake was, he'd put it on the wrong side of the wound. Propped against a tree, he watched himself die, because there was nobody else around.

As Peter said one afternoon at the Las Delicias—he and his horse had dragged themselves cut and bleeding into the corral: "You can get up someday, take a ride into those rocks"—he flung his hand at Chiltipiñes canyon—"and never come back. Nobody would ever know where to find you. If you don't want to live with that possibility, don't live on a ranch."

Some of the noblest ranchers I knew were men who'd rarely set foot in a church. But I'd seen them plunge their horses into a treacherous river, just to save a cow. Or seen them snowshoe in a subzero gale for miles, searching for a neighbor who might or might not be lost. The danger of it, the risk of death? The subject didn't seem to come up with such men. Or, perhaps they'd made their peace with the possibility, in their own kind of way.

It was that peace which I wanted very much to find. And to do so meant a humbling. But out here in the enormity of nature, I was up against something bigger than I. I couldn't pound nature into a small box or a group of symbols. It behaved the way it wanted, sweeping me along on a force that I had either to accept or always to fear.

In retraining our "coping" mechanism, certain practical lessons had to be learned. In Arizona, for example, we'd never reach under anything, never walk into any dark underbrush. Still, at times our vigilance would lapse. Late one afternoon, Teddy was hurrying down to milk her cow when she heard from inside the barn the telltale sound of a ruptured pipe, spraying water. Because the loss of a drop of water was a super-emergency in the desert, she flung open the tin door and rushed toward . . . no, recoiled! An arm-thick rattler was coiled just beneath her foot, his tongue darting out in full striking position. And what he wanted to strike was Teddy's beloved cat, Mamma, who was teasing him a few inches from his fangs.

With a scream, Teddy lurched back and flung the door shut. But then, in a logic known only to the maternal instinct, she realized that Mamma, who was old and slow after her countless litters, was about to get killed. With this, Teddy flung open the door again, thrust herself down to within inches of the snake, and snatched Mamma away. No, the snake didn't strike. Probably he couldn't believe that any human could be so stupid. Once Teddy had Mamma in her clutches—and because they were both alone at the ranch that afternoon—she did what was necessary, particularly when we had grandchildren often toddling around the barns. She returned with one of my quail guns and blew the snake apart.

Well, I thought, that was one less that would come slinking around where the people lived. Yet, a few weeks later, the leaky toilet in my office overflowed, and to mop the floor, we had to roll up the rug. I was working on something at the time and, in my usual absentmindedness, forgot about unrolling the rug again. Early one morning, we had a small ranch business conference in my office, three people and two chairs (we were a very small business!). Peter, having no place to park himself, lay on the rolled rug. Suddenly he exploded in a howl. Something had been writhing under his shoulders. When he flipped back the rug, a rattler was about four inches from his face.

The thought couldn't help crossing my mind: suppose on some energetic morning I'd finally decided to reach down and open the rug? Well, chalk it up to a good learning experience for a messy man. *Leave things as they are!*

When the realization dawned on us that we were at least an hour and a half from the nearest antivenom, we bought a snake kit and put it in our refrigerator. And in Wyoming, we kept a stretcher rolled up in the barn. But what for, really?

Once, in Wyoming, when Pete was about fifteen, he and I were breaking a wild young colt. When it became too dark to see, I told Pete to unbridle the colt, who'd had enough anyway, and I drifted off to bed. About an hour later, I was struck by some instinct pervasive enough to make me bolt up in bed. I ran to the window and shouted for Pete, down at the stable.

What answered me was a moan. He was lying there, semiconscious. The colt had kicked him in the chest, broken his ribs. An inch or two lower, in the stomach, could have killed him. The same summer, a horse wrangler I knew was kicked in the belly and died on the spot.

Well, I could sigh, we got out of that one. And what parent doesn't have his moments of terror and feeling of helplessness? "Put them in God's hands," Teddy used to say. And God certainly had his hands full with Tom, one night long before in Wyoming.

On a December afternoon, we'd decided to take an innocent family outing, running up to the forest on our snowmachines and cutting our Christmas tree. It was so unseasonably warm that Tom wore only a Levi jacket. After we'd cut the tree, Tom and Roberto, a Mexican youngster who was living with us, chose to stay up in the nine-thousand-foot-high basin and do some snowmachining. I kept asking Tom: "You're sure you know how to start this machine without flooding it?" Oh, absolutely. Then Teddy and I put on our skis, and in snow that was ten feet deep, tracked down to the ranch house five miles away.

We'd no sooner gotten home than the wind began to howl. In less than an hour, the temperature dropped forty degrees to well below zero. Across the ranch swept a dreaded whiteout, swirling up the snow until the horizon was gone, and certainly any sense of direction. In whiteouts like these, ranchers have learned to unhitch their work teams, grab onto their tails, and on the hard-packed cattle-feeding routes, let the horses guide them home. But what about Tom and Roberto? We realized they had neither skis nor snowshoes. Without them, if they tried to take a step in those drifts, they'd plunge in up to their armpits.

By the time night fell, they still weren't home, and we,

frantically, were trying to churn our creaking Sno-Cat up the hills to where we thought they might be. On the first real grade, the cursed Cat with its badly missing engine spun out in a groan of exhaust smoke and buried itself in a drift. We knew we couldn't go any farther, nor could we find our way on skis.

At that exact moment, the boys saw our lights. As predicted, Tom had flooded the snowmachine so thoroughly that after kicking it and cursing it enough times, he finally had to abandon it. But to his credit, and Roberto's they didn't panic. When they discovered that every step they took would only bury them head-deep in snow, they evolved a technique for rolling themselves like logs on top of the snow, and thus they covered all the miles needed without quite freezing to death.

Tom got out of that one with something verging on pneumonia. As for little Roberto, by the time we found his scarf and knitted cap the next spring, he had fled back to Zacatecas, where it seldom even rains. As a demure little Chinese girl said, shivering in our ranch house—she'd flown direct from Formosa into a similar blizzard: "Your country, Mr. Carney, is very cold experience."

The cold of fear, naturally; routine, mundane actions that go suddenly wrong: the horse that has jumped over a thousand badger holes for Teddy, until the one she misses, knocks her out so thoroughly that for an hour she can't remember where or who she is. All the kids who've chopped all the firewood, until the most coordinated boy we've ever had working—manages to get the ax in the kneecap. Or why exactly did the hand put a tractor into the wrong gear, so that it jumped forward and plunged with its driver into a ten-foot ditch?

Accidents will happen, boys will be boys. But when the boy is an oldish man, and now pretty much alone, he learns a few simple things. When an old man rides a young, unbroken horse somewhere out in nineteen square miles, he prudently tells someone at the ranch his exact course for the buckout that might follow. And when a car goes down the lonely hundred-mile road to town, and doesn't come back on an approximate schedule, we go out and look.

In those years in the Altar Valley, we also had another element to contend with. When the drug traffic was at its peak, we often used to feel that we were like noncombatants in a war zone. We were pawns in the deadly game that was going on. The big empty border desert was twitching with strange noises. But we didn't really *see* anybody. And if we had, if we stumbled onto them, they had their sights set on a bigger target, we hoped. Once, in a lonely arroyo, I found seven hundred pounds of marijuana, carefully stuffed into backpacks—hidden here, no doubt waiting for a pickup. But the envoy didn't choose to appear when I stumbled onto his loot. Maybe he was coming that night.

Or who, I often asked, left a bunch of empty transistor radio boxes hidden in the mesquite down near our mail box? The Border Patrol explained it when it picked them up. The transistors were popular trade goods for drugs. "Sometimes," the agent grinned, "they trade their heroin for automatic weapons, but in that case you wouldn't have found any boxes, maybe just some oily rags."

But, throughout those years, a lurking awareness was building: when am I going to blunder into somebody's loot, when he doesn't want me there?

Then, one morning when I was out quail hunting, in an arroyo that was far from any road on the ranch, one of my companions, a youngster from the East, cried: "Hey, Mr. Carney, there's a car in here!"

Car? Couldn't be! No way to drive into such a rocky place.

Yet, there it was, as if deposited by helicopter. Parked and locked, twelve feet down into the arroyo, was a new yellow Mustang, no license on it. When the Border Patrolmen arrived, they broke into the car with a coat hanger, read the factory serial number into their hand radios. Chillingly, within moments, the DAWN (Drug Alert Warning Network) computer was hammering back from Washington. The vehicle, stolen, was wanted by both the Chicago and the Kansas City police. It was a Mafia courier car, the agents said, placed there in the arroyo to stand by and pick up a load of heroin.

"But how the devil," I said, "did anybody even know an arroyo existed way back here? You can't see it from any road you can drive."

The agent smiled. "They fly the valley. And they've also got the latest government aerial photo maps of every acre in it."

One afternoon later that week, I was up breaking a filly in the lonely San Miguel canyon. Because the filly was giving me some trouble, I took her on a punishment trip that was a gallop up a narrow sandy trail. After we'd veered in and out of mesquite trees for a mile or so, I turned her around and let her walk slowly back down the same trail.

At one lone tree, she snorted and almost jumped out from under me. Then I saw what she saw: two human legs protruding from beneath the tree. "What the hell?" I cried.

A nondescript-looking man of about thirty emerged. "Oh," he grunted. "This your ranch, huh?"

Shades of the drug agent in the driveway. I said, yes, it was my ranch, and could he explain how he happened to be lying under a tree up at six thousand feet?

Sure, he could explain. A helicopter dropped him. Then he mumbled something about a mining company he was working for. They were prospecting uranium.

"Where's your equipment?"

"Ah, I don't know. They just told me to pick up some rocks."

Patiently, I got him to repeat the name of the mining company, and then advised him to pick up his feet right down the canyon, even showing him the exact route to get to the highway.

Back at the house I called the Border Patrol, which punched its computers again and found no record of any such mining company in either the U.S. or Canada. Maybe he was from the Soviet Union.

At any rate, whoever he was, he never came back. Eventually, the drug business seemed to wind down, and as with the snakes and the rest of it, we put it out of our minds.

Then very early one morning Teddy and I pulled onto the road toward Tucson. I happened to glance in the mirror and, like the smuggling night with Refugia, saw a Border Patrol car cruising slowly. Its top lights were flashing, but in a leisurely, polite signal, not like some angry traffic cop, of whom we had none on that lonely road. I pulled over and a friendly agent peered into the window. He explained, almost apologetically, that the following day, the patrol would be working out in the valley—"running a little maneuver" was the way he put it. He just wanted to check again what vehicles we had at the ranch, and who might be driving them. Of course, he already had the list in his hand, because the patrol in those days came into the ranch almost daily. I think I gave him the name of a new driver. He thanked us, and we drove on.

If there was a "maneuver" the next day, I certainly didn't see any of it, or care. Once, I did hear the patrol's Cessna humming over the ranch, but it was always doing that, searching the mesquite for wetbacks. After lunch, as usual, I got into the truck and went down to get my cherished mail. Before I even reached the mail box, a car drifted slowly up the road toward me. When we pulled even with each other, I stopped as I always do, hoping to save some wanderer an eight-mile trip up to the house, only to find he was in the wrong valley, or the people he wanted had moved to Texas.

The car was a sedan, clearly a rental type, brand new and shiny, and in it were four men. The driver was an Anglo with a heavily jowled face, a man in his forties, I imagined. Seated beside him was a sulky looking Mexican type, and in the back seat were another Mexican of the same mold and a huge black. They were all somewhat younger than the driver, darkly dressed in western-type suits and bolo ties. "You live here, do you?" the driver asked. "What's your name?"

I told him, and at the same time asked what he happened to be looking for, on a private road.

He didn't answer directly. They were all watching me, in a somewhat bored, heavy-lidded way. The driver's arm hung on the steering wheel and he slowly lifted one forefinger. "Now, that ranch up by the mountains, who lives there?"

I gave him the owner's name. Then he drifted his finger north, and he got that owner too. Finally he asked me about a rancher to the south of me. Did I know him?

When I said I did, he grinned. "Yeah. Well, he's a friend of ours. We'll go down there. We're going to cut some firewood."

"You what?"

"Saw up a few trees. You know, winter coming." Then they glanced at each other and chuckled.

Aw, come on, fellas, I thought. Out here in your city suits, bolo ties, not a sign of a chain saw, and you're going to cut mesquite?

"Okay," I said, "good luck." And by the time I got home with my mail, I was smiling myself, particularly when I described it to Teddy. In my years as a noncombatant in the drug trade, my research had led me to interview perhaps a dozen characters exactly like these. "Why," I explained to Teddy, "they're right out of the mold. They're DEA cops all the way. The driver is probably out of some big-city narco squad, and the younger guys are these street-smart toughs who do the undercover. I'll bet I've seen five kids that look just like that black, or the Mexicans, down at DEA headquarters."

"Are you really sure?"

"Of course I am. Why, to pull that phony firewood-cutting routine on me, that's a typical cop brushoff."

"Yes, but...don't you think you ought to check with the patrol?"

Just as I'd expected, I got the agent-dispatcher on the phone, told him my little tale. Casually, he took down what few facts I had. So that I wouldn't sound too much like a cry-wolf, I mentioned that I knew they had some sort of training maneuver out here today. These DEA people were obviously part of it. The dispatcher said, "I wasn't aware of anything going on. But we'll check it out."

"Does that satisfy you?" I said to Teddy.

"Well, it's always better to be sure."

What was not better, however, was my being awakened before seven the next morning by a loud rapping on the kitchen door. Just beyond it stood two Border Patrol cars with the motors running, and more men in green suits than I'd noticed in a long time. "Mr. Carney," said one agent quietly, "what was the make of that car and the plate on it?"

Well, I fumbled, I hadn't noticed. Some Hertz-type sedan, never thought about a plate, particularly after talking to those obvious DEA agents.

His lips tightened and there was just an imperceptible shake of his head. "Too bad you didn't get a better description. We've checked out DEA, Treasury, Arizona Strike Force. They didn't belong to any of them, nor to us. Those were the people we wanted."

There was another kind of visitor we always enjoyed having at the ranches: old friends who'd come to hunt and fish with us. To me, they were a beloved touch of the past, and often a mirror in which to see the change I was struggling for in my own life. Most of my friends had come from the competitive hurry of urban business. Just because they flew on a jet for a few hours, pulled on hunting clothes, and parachuted into the nineteenth century was no reason to suppose that their inner time clocks would have been put on hold.

I could sympathize with their predicament now, having spent so many years trying to slow myself. Thus, when a film-director friend jetted over to hunt quail on the Las Delicias, I should have known what was coming. Here was a man who at the flick of a finger could control casts of thousands, burn the city of Paris on the back lot, or ram a jet through a papier-mâché skyscraper. And now, to ram some little quail around on a forgotten desert? What a comedown! I must admit I was impressed when he told me he was using a famous actor's shotgun, given him as a gift. But then my heart sank when my friend, like some imperial majesty of film, robed himself in a baby-blue cashmere jumpsuit. On his feet were expensive ankle-high "boots," so soft and suede-y that they were clearly intended for a desert like, say, Rodeo Drive. I warned him that we'd have to do a lot of walking on rocks for these birds.

Not to worry, he purred. Okay, I thought: you're a big, tough boy who plays four sets of tennis every night after leaving the studio. Maybe you're in shape for this. So off we went, up and down arroyos, following my relentless little dog, Kiku. My friend hurled himself gamely at the challenge, during the first few hours trudging on, sweating profusely. Once in a while he'd lose his footing. His gun barrel would flail around perilously, so finally I took the precaution of assigning him the other side of an arroyo where we would be buffered from each other by heavy mesquite. I'd hear him fire, then silence. "Get it?" I would shout. No answer. After enough blasting, Kiku finally trotted back in my direction, and her eyes had kind of a shudder in them, as if to say: Who is this guy who can blow away so many of my beautiful points?

The arroyo we were walking was about three miles long and filled with birds. After each cannonade from the other side, I no longer had to ask the result, because every shot was now followed by some rich show-business expletive. Finally, a pair of birds thundered up in an opening between us. I could see them whistling away, silver-blue little comets, too far for me, but my friend shot. Boom! Boom! Then: "I got them, by God!"

"You did?" I echoed.

"Damn right. They fell, just over there." He jabbed the famous actor's gun toward a sandy little basin, with only some cactus in it and very little cover.

"Well, good," I said. "Kiku ought to be able to find them then," and I put her off to the fetch, despite the fact that I'd seen those two quail flying unscathed about a half mile away. But, I felt sorry for him and had to go through the motions. Anyway, Kiku could always use some hunt-dead practice. So I walked beyond him and engrossed myself in helping the "retrieve."

A moment later, I heard a wail, then an awful howl. "Goddammit! Sonofabitch!" I spun around to see a lump of blue cashmere rolling in the desert, then arms and legs were flinging out of it, lashing, kicking like a scalded baby. When I ran over, my friend was on his back, pounding his feet in the dust, his cashmere festooned with prickling balls of cholla cactus. Apparently he'd stepped on the first one, then kicked at it for its offense to his person. When he tried to slap at the balls, they were sticking in his fingers and wrists. "Just lie absolutely still," I said to this baby-blue porcupine. "Come on now, quit fighting it!" Then, I picked up two flat rocks and,

perhaps like his barber at the studio plucking his eyebrows, slowly squeezed each cholla ball between the rocks
until I had finally "groomed" him clean. That pretty well
ended the hunt. As we walked back toward the truck, he
was still plucking cholla spines out of his butt.

How often, too, I'd take friends out duck hunting in the
loops of the Green River, where it wound through the
ranch. One favorite area is an old river channel, shaped
like a horseshoe, and because it has become a rich
backwater, the ducks breed here. By the time the Wyoming skies have chilled over in the fall, the horseshoe loop
has enough mallard and widgeon in it so that when
something ignites them, they boil up into the sky, great
squadrons whistling and crisscrossing overhead in a
splendor that makes your heart tremble.

Unlike the usual eastern or Mississippi Valley duck
hunting, we used no decoys. This was Indian-style jump
shooting, and it required perfect timing. Year after year,
I'd drop off my hunters at various points near the
horseshoe, and give them explicit, whispered instructions
that once they saw my truck stop, each party was to walk at
a crouch across the yellowed hay meadows, moving very
slowly and quietly, taking advantage of a few willows as
cover, and finally crawling on his belly to the edge of the
high bluff. If everybody did it right, we'd all arrive in
position simultaneously. The ducks would not have been
able to see us until that moment, screened as we were by
the high river bank. Thus, in this perfect sneak, they
would explode upward, and by old habit fly around the
horseshoe, following the course of the water until every
party of hunters had had more than enough shots.

The perfect sneak. Yet, in all the years with my city
hunter friends, we rarely made it work. Invariably,
there'd always be some charging, competitive type in the
group who insisted on taking a hurrying shortcut to the
river bank, then thrust himself up as erect and gleaming as

a totem pole. One long-necked mallard duck would cock his wary head, then leap up quacking, and off go the fireworks. I'd usually find myself standing out in some willow bog, far from the river. Over us would tower pillars of ducks at least five hundred feet in the sky. I'd hear only one or two shots along the river and they were usually misses from the hunter who had to get in there first. Kiku would look up at me and we'd both groan, as if to say, couldn't they ever wait?

With fishing, the fury of getting and spending became even more discouraging to me. Up in the beaver ponds on the higher drainage of the ranch, I knew there were plenty of trout—I loved them like brothers because I'd lugged a lot of them in there myself; nursed them as fingerlings, trapped them in tiny side creeks, and brought them to a better home.

So again, as we'd approach the ponds, I'd give a little lecture to the effect that these trout fed very slowly, usually on small nymphs. Often they'd be right under the beaver dam where the fisherman's feet were going to be. And because the trout loved dark, shady places that protected them from the hovering osprey, my friend would have to go in silently, study the pond for just such cover areas, and then, with Polaroid glasses to break the glare, look into the water quietly and carefully. There'd be a good chance he might see a lunker-size trout cruising the shallows like a slow, lumbering shark. The trout would want a nymph. My friend had one on. "Fine," I'd whisper. "Give your rod a tiny flick of your wrist." The nymph will drop out no more than six feet from you, sometimes as close as a yard. The lunker simply opens his mouth, takes it, and swims away. And, most important, *wait* those one or two agonizing seconds after you've seen the faint swirl—only then, strike the fish! Now, he's got it, deep in his jaw.

As many times as I gave that lecture, my old friend would clump right up on the beaver dam, and while he was still floundering around on the slippery logs, he'd begin to whip out his shiny new line. He hadn't *looked* at the nature of the pond, hadn't waited to get any feel of it. Instead, he'd now be lacing out one of those expensive, looping casts he'd learned during the winter at fly-fishing school. And it wasn't even a cast, but a whistling, lashing line in the false-casting stage, that is, the action you perform when you're trying to dry off a fly in the air so it will float.

But this fly was supposed to sink! A nymph comes *up* from the bottom. Not only that, I'd begged my friend: never false-cast! You'd spook the close fish, the big one next to the bank. They'd think your whipping line was the flash of some predator's wings.

And what of the little unimpressive cast of a yard to six feet? No, it never proved enough for my friend. He wanted action, performance, results; and, of course, his method would get none. Neither would my hurrying city companions who'd rush down to the bank of the Green River in the gray dawn of morning (usually the first morning after they'd arrived). Get out there, get it done, get the numbers. Usually, I wouldn't even be out of bed when I'd hear them hollering to each other along the river: "What kind of fly you using? Mine isn't worth a damn!"

By the time they'd straggled in for breakfast, dour and empty-handed (some of them downright sulky about it), I'd try to explain that a fish was about like anybody else. He didn't like to get out and work in the chilled dawn, before the water had warmed up enough for any hatch or feed activity to take place. Wait, just lie doggo until the sun had risen to about high noon. "Sun?" my friends would echo. "You can't catch trout in bright sunlight!" Any fool knew that, back in Maine or Michigan or wherever. And so my friends would gobble down their breakfast and rush out to have at it again.

Even the way they ate—yes, I noticed it and I remembered, because I used to do the same thing myself, wolf it down. I'd gobble breakfast as I hurried for the commuting train. At a business luncheon, I'd often be so busy chattering and negotiating I could barely taste what I put into my mouth. The most boring thing in the world seemed to be eating with slow, deliberate savor.

Yet, in Wyoming cow camps or Mexican adobes, I'd shared many a meal where no one talked. Indeed, our eyes didn't even meet. How restful it was to sit there—slowed, silenced, unpenetrated.

Gradually over the years, as I watched the reactions of my hunting and fishing friends, I realized that an important change was occurring in me. My time clock had slowed to such a point, my rhythm so different from theirs, that I began to feel attuned more to the quarry than to the stalker. I wanted the birds or the fish to win, and not the hunter.

In my research on *Crazy Horse*, I'd come on evidence that before the Indians killed their game, and certainly after the kill, they would offer a prayer of atonement for having destroyed a living thing, as if it were a part of themselves. Though the game was needed for food or clothing, its death was still something to be mourned, a removal from the whole. And, what I was finding tragic in my friends was their ignorance of this concept. To them, game or fish were numbers, ego exploits, too soon forgotten, often not even enjoyed as food, and sometimes not eaten at all.

But in my routine that had developed over the years— writing in the morning, and then out to hunt, fish, or ride in the afternoons—my solitary forays into nature served as a period of reconnection. The look of a stream, the flash of a fish seeking cover, the wariness of a mallard in a slough brought me not only a physical release but a spiritual one. Thus, like a beta blocker used in medicine, a form of

blocker seemed to rise in my nervous system until I
realized I didn't really want to take that duck or fish. I
wanted to leave him where he belonged. My joy had been
to participate with him, in stalking and reaching him in
his world.

I found more and more that my best hunts were those in
which I'd spent hours trudging the desert, and had only
one or two birds to bring home. Getting there, it seemed
now, was not half the fun, but most of it.

There never was a better duck or quail shot than old
Fuzzy-Face, not that I've seen. That is, when he was
right; and he was always at his hair-trigger best in Mexico,
which he loved. How many great hunts we had down
there, with him stumping along like some barrel-chested
Hemingway, whom he did resemble and perhaps imi-
tated. Hemingway might have been a wizard with the
written word, but Fuzzy-Face was a raconteur in the
bawdiest tradition, the campfire standup comedian. After
he'd drunk most people into their sleeping bags, and there
was only a hardcore few of us listening to his last stories,
he'd jerk out his harmonica and begin playing us the great
ballads of the Mexican Revolution. "Valentina" was
always one of his favorites. He would then knock the spit
out of his harmonica, and we'd join in as he bellowed what
he always used as the finale: "Adios, muchachos, compañeros de mi vida..." ("Goodbye, boys, companions of
my life").

The greatest love Fuzzy-Face had in him was his love
for the little people of the world. They broke him up, and
he, though of a wildly different background, came through
to them as totally genuine. Lumpy old cowboys, rummy
hunting guides, and God knows how many Mexican taxi
drivers followed him around like adoring bird dogs. He
used Mexican taxis to haul us out to the duck lakes. One of

his raunchiest drivers, Alfredo, had a dimwitted younger brother about twelve. Since we had no dog, Fuzzy-Face trained Alfredo as a handler. Let some fat pintail crumple and splash down in a lake fifty yards from shore, Fuzzy-Face would say, "Bueno, Alfredo, cojele"—the Spanish equivalent for "fetch." Proudly, Alfredo would turn to his younger brother, give him the "away" signal, and the poor kid would plunge bravely into the freezing water, thrashing around out there, hardly knowing how to swim. But after he'd been "shot over" with enough birds, Fuzzy-Face and Alfredo had him responding to right-hand and lefthand signals; in fact, the kid often brought the birds back with their necks in his teeth.

Alfredo also had a fourteen-year-old sister whom he tried to make a *regalito* ("little gift of") to Fuzzy-Face. But perhaps the crowning achievement of their hunts to-gether was one shoot we were planning out at a so-called legendary lake near Navajoa, Sonora. Alfredo's advance billing was so glowing that a young American couple from Rolling Rock, Pennsylvania, overheard and asked to join us. Fuzzy-Face had an ingrained distaste for fancy people, and when these two reported for duty at dawn, both wearing slinky Abercrombie hunting clothes and carry-ing feather-light, gilt-engraved Purdy shotguns, I noticed Fuzzy-Face wink diabolically at Alfredo. All the way out in the taxi, the nice young couple told us of the splendid shoots they were used to back home. Club stuff, beauti-fully controlled lady and gentleman hunting. Then, we bailed out of the taxi at the appropriate mesquite thicket and began what seemed to me an incredibly long, infantry-type belly crawl, our shotguns cradled in our elbows as we wriggled like worms over yards and yards of desert. Fuzzy-Face was whispering gruff orders, enjoying himself tremendously as the dudes dirtied up their Aber-crombies and began to sweat in the dawning sun. Finally, as we neared the dam that shielded the fabled lake from us,

Fuzzy-Face beckoned at Alfredo and whispered in evil Spanish: "Bueno, compadre, tell 'em how we do it down here."

Alfredo pushed archly up on his knees and firmly tapped the gentleman and lady shooters on their tailored shoulders. "Hey, mister, missus," he whispered in his execrable English, "do not choot de ducks on de water!"

Sluicing? On the water?

The unforgivable sin!... and from Rolling Rock, yet! The poor young fellow and his wife were so aghast at the accusation that they sat gaping while Fuzzy-Face gave the over-the-top signal. The rest of us went scrambling up the dam—to what?

Desert.

Apparently, in the days since Alfredo had last visited the lake, this pintail paradise, some friendly peon had drained all the water out of it, and we stood looking at an expanse of cracked, dry earth, with one lonely burro trying to graze in the middle of it.

I still think Fuzzy-Face knew it was dry all along, but he'd gotten in his shot at the "fancies," and that was all that mattered to him: loving the little people, and chuckling at their pomp when they tried to be big ones.

On the way home from that trip, Fuzzy-Face and I stopped for the night in the bordertown of Mexicali. The only place that advertised a vacancy was a garlic-smelling dump over which blazed a sign: "Hilton Motel." To a sleepy Mexican desk clerk, Fuzzy-Face exclaimed: "Aha! What a beautiful place you have here! Don't tell me by some chance this motel is connected to the great Hilton chain?"

The clerk drew himself up proudly and said: "We are the same, señor, in name only."

But there was none the same as Fuzzy-Face, not for me, at least. I missed him after I'd moved to Wyoming. Oh, we still hunted and fished a few times, when schedules permitted. And once, too, he'd called me from some obscure shrimp port in Mexico. He wanted to tell me about the shark fishermen. He'd apparently fallen in with a whole village of them, and was all excited about doing a film story on their lives. But there was only one hitch. The shark fishermen refused to be photographed. They were hard, flinty *marineros* who didn't take to outsiders, and that bothered Fuzzy-Face because these were his kind of boys. Finally one day, as they dourly skinned a giant seagoing shark on their boat deck, Fuzzy-Face looked down at the gaping mouth with its awesome rows of teeth and said, "Cut that thing out and give it to me, will you?"

Puzzled, one of the fishermen hacked away, and after he'd gotten the mouth loose, his curiosity overcame him. "Why," he grunted, "would the señor want this?"

"To make it into a pillow," Fuzzy-Face answered, "for my mother-in-law."

In the vicarious delight of that idea, the fishermen howled, and from then on Fuzzy-Face was one of them, as always.

But where I really missed Fuzzy-Face the most, I suppose, was when other "fancies," wandering summer soldiers, descended on the ranch to be taken fishing.

One of these, who seemed at the outset to be begging for one of Fuzzy-Face's harpoons, was a grumpy old codger whom a friend had sent my way. He called up and complained about how terrible the fishing was in Wyoming. Therefore, what about his coming over and going with me out on my river? The rumor was, I was supposed to have some fish.

I said, lying in my teeth, fine (I didn't have anything else to do, which he had inferred), so, the next afternoon he came stumping in with a gruff, get-at-it manner, and we put my boat into the Green River. I didn't even bring my rod, because it had seemed evident from our first conversation that I was expected to be the guide, pay my dues so to speak for not being back in an office in the city. The old man would jab his rod tip at me, which was a signal that he'd just lashed off another fly in his tight, angry casts. I'd tie him on a new one, give my best recommendations and most enthusiastic you-should-have-been-here-last-week stories. We'd float through some deep moody bend where I *knew* there were fish. He'd lash, swear, smoke cigarettes. Nothing.

Then, purpling storm clouds rose above us; everything was sluggish, expectant. From the hay meadows we were sliding through, mosquitoes came swarming. "If you can try to relax to them," I'd suggest, "they don't seem to bite you as much." He'd keep beating at the back of his neck, slapping his hands. Finally he tossed his rod in the bottom of the boat. "There's no fish here."

"They're certainly not doing much."

He grunted darkly; then his eyes began to sweep the hay meadows with their moose-proof log cribs where we stored the bales; he swept further, down to the slouching corrals and homesteader log buildings: here lay dull gleams of abandoned machinery flung into the grass, and a red tractor that my foreman was repairing. "This place," the old man snapped. "Why, you couldn't possibly make a nickel out of it. They're all the same, ranches, damn losing proposition, that's what."

While he glowered at me as if I were a balance sheet, I suppose I stammered out the usual: sure, ranching was tough, but we did manage to get a lifestyle out of it.

"Hell," he said. "You couldn't afford to be doing this at all, if you didn't have an outside income. That's the truth of it."

I felt my lips tighten. I wanted to paste it up there in front of him, because that's what he wanted. Yes, I had outside income. But I had also earned some; so spool off the film credits and the books, run 'em up the flagpole. Defend my sense of worth, measured on the dollar. That was the old reflex: fight back with a hatred of the money-objectification of my world. But for some reason—maybe the new book I was writing, the trying—I said nothing. A wind riffled across the boat; the clouds that threatened didn't come over; they began to break and scatter against the fortresses of the Wind River mountains. The sun slanted under them, penetrating the water. "You can see the fish now," I told him. "Why don't you try this stretch from here into the house? It's the best water we've got."

He nodded. He'd made his point, summed me up. Now, he might as well catch a fish. As we slid past the shadows of the barns, he managed to catch several, jerking them into the boat, never even looking at them once they were dead. "How many is that?" he'd ask. I'd tell him. We'd count the numbers. When I finally slid the boat onto the bank, down the bluff from the house, he made no move to get out. He just looked back at the stretch of river, amber now in the last sun.

"You know," he murmured, "my life. Stocks and bonds. Rode the train into Wall Street thirty years. Made a lot of money. Did it all myself...and hated every goddamn minute of it!" When he turned to me, his face had crumbled. He brushed at his eyes. "Ah, hell," he said. "Let's get a drink," and he went stumping up the bank, not even offering to take his fish.

Well, the years passed, and there were other fonder companions with whom I often did hunt or fish. Two of them were even older friends than Fuzzy-Face, and like him, we were all similar in our backgrounds: Ivy League educations, World War II service. We'd managed early to amass the usual symbols of happiness: lovely houses in a suburb of a major city, memberships in the clubs we'd wanted; trophies from the games and the stuffed birds; kids in what they called the right schools; a sense of identity and importance in our communities, business, and at home. We had wives who loved us, and wanted our fulfillment as their goal. As the nation wrangled through the Cold War, and felt the earth shocks of Cubas, assassinations and integrations, college rebellion, Vietnam, these men had their rebels as we all did, and one even had a marine son in Vietnam. But their lives went on— sure, sometimes with bitching about politics, interest rates, inflation, occasionally mourning a world that seemed to be discarding us, flinging away a victory we'd won, calling our values into doubt. Yet even in the questioning we all feel in the middle of life, these men, I thought, were simply plowing ahead, doing what they'd been trained for, doing it well: finding their worth in their economic success.

The first of these friends was a venture capitalist who'd worked hard and built his own firm. Once I'd suggested that he might want to put some money into land, out where we were in Wyoming, so we could fish together. He wrote me that he'd dearly love to, but unfortunately right then, with a market setback, he was heavily committed, and so were some of his friends, gambling with him. He kept staying later and later at the office, hanging in there, waiting for the game to turn around. One day, during a tennis game, he sagged onto the court and within hours was dead of a massive heart attack.

The second friend, who'd gone to Princeton as I had, was also in the financial business. He'd made millions earlier, and had spent them with gusto. When the game turned around on him—it was much harder. He was older, and could see that he had little time left to make up his losses. At that point he started to despair. Because he loved being number one, always the best at everything, owning the best of everything, he couldn't stand to see them taken away, the things. Knowing his depression and feeling of failure, Teddy and I both wrote him, begging him to see himself as the unique man he was. Teddy's letter was still in his pocket when the chauffeur found him, dead by his own gun in his garage.

The third friend had been a naval officer in Pearl Harbor during the attack. For much of his postwar life, he had suffered from tuberculosis, which he had contracted in the Pacific. Finally, he simply decided to opt out of the money game, and enjoy what he could give to the world, which was mainly his genuine, lovable self. But it still wasn't enough, or so he thought. Because he didn't earn, and was no longer in the chase, he decided that by the lights that had raised him, he had failed. Teddy and I both sensed this, so we also begged him to buy some land in Wyoming, sell out in the city—his kids were raised and gone—come join us. Then unbeknownst to me, Teddy invited him and his wife to a surprise birthday party for me. He accepted eagerly and was delighted to be coming to the Arizona ranch. We might even shoot some quail.

The same day he went out and bought me a birthday present. Then the man, who was Fuzzy-Face, returned to his study, lay down neatly like the good hunter he was, and destroyed himself.

At each of the deaths, I was stunned, sickened. And then, as I reflected on them, violently angered. Because the enemy that killed these men was my enemy too. It was the way we had been raised, the values we had been bred to revere. Money, power, things—in whatever order you put them. Control of your life; only success matters; what you did, what you earned. If you began to fail, and worse, took others with you, there was no out: failure was death, and their hearts seemed to be saying as much as when they stopped.

With my second friend, who had made and spent his millions, the drug of things, money, material success had addicted him; without them, he had no sense of worth, no reason to live.

But old Fuzzy-Face, game and gamy, *had* tried to battle it out, even though he knew that just being himself, a superb and generous man, was not deemed repayment in kind. By opting out of our work ethic and its materialist goal, he had sinned against what we held sacred.

I was guiding some old friends on a float trip down the Green River. We'd pulled the boat onto a sandbar, because my fishermen had an urge to stretch their legs, have a beer, and work a deep pool that looked inviting. I lay out on the warm sand and watched them. Upriver there was a splashing. A cow moose had plunged into the water, followed by her leggy, amber calf, about the size of a pony. Spooked by the unaccustomed noise, a golden-eye duck, followed by a brood of tiny, furry ducklings, scurried away from the bank and paddled downstream. But when she caught sight of us and realized the threat we were, she went into her broken-wing act and began flapping wild circles in the river, trying to get us to pursue her until her ducklings would have time to hide somewhere in the tall grass.

"What a place!" exclaimed one of my friends. "I can't say I've ever had a more wonderful morning, anywhere!"

I pushed up on the sand and saw that the older of my two companions had stopped fishing. He was standing above me, looking at the battlements of the Wind River mountains thrusting up just beyond us. Closer, the hay meadows, ripe for cutting, were swaying in a faint breeze that rippled the crystal river water into showers of diamonds. Then, slowly, he squatted beside me, this big man from a big city, an important man. "Tell me something," he said quietly. "Do you ever miss it?"

"Miss what?" I asked.

"Oh, being back in the city, I suppose. The people, excitement of it. Things going on..."

"Well, sure," I said. "Sometimes."

I don't know if that was the answer he expected. His face didn't register anything. But then, because he was a fine, sensitive old man, I felt obliged to frame it for him better, and no doubt for myself too, because this was the question so often asked of me. And my answer, I'm afraid, usually came out like a foreign language, losing much in translation.

Miss it? Of course! What active, gregarious human being in the twentieth century wouldn't miss the seductions of fascinating people, comforts, the stimulations of all our sophisticated media, the chase, the pulse, the being where it was happening? Very few of those titillating sounds managed to creep up the long curving bends into the pastoral silence of the ages on the Green River.

But when I'd been used to hearing them for so much of my life, could I let them go? That's the question he was really asking. Because I wanted to answer him as honestly as I could, I had to say, yes, I can let them go.

But *only* if I put something else in their place. Because there was a definite void here.

The stimuli of the urban milieu and the concomitant reward structure has been so deeply sculptured into most of us by our culture that we find it almost as hard to lop off as, say, a right arm. Indeed, because that conditioning is such an integral part of us—we have invested so much of our best self in it—it is foolhardy and certainly counterproductive to attempt to cut with it. One friend of mine once "went western" to the degree that he tried to turn himself into the moldiest corral-talkin' cowhand that ever came down the trail. Well, of course, it didn't work. Nor did it for the Peace Corps girls from New York who went out to Ponape in the Pacific and insisted on swimming bare-breasted like the native women. The natives were scandalized. They wanted the American girls to be what they were, and stop trying to posture their way into another identity.

Therefore, if you have to be what you are—in my case, a city bred—no, you don't give that up, because you can't. But you do begin to make a slow transformation which, I think, has several phases.

The first is the comparison. As I told my questioner in the river that morning, my antidote for "missing it" was to plunge back into it from time to time. Sure, I loved a morning paper, a vital business luncheon, a good movie, good play, glittering dinner party—enjoyed them as much as the next man when my writing work would occasionally return me to New York and Los Angeles.

But, as I quickly added to my companion that morning in the river, after two or three days of the urban chase and its surfeit, I'd always start feeling an unmistakable sense of *deja vu*, as if I'd done this several decades ago, and had already seen the ending. Then, in the urban noise—lying in bed some night, trying to sleep in the din of horns, sirens, and television laugh tracks—well, if this were stimulation, and surely my nerves were keyed up to a pitch—I'd find myself longing only for the big silence again, the open sweep of the sagebrush or the mesquite, my new ocean now, to rock me to sleep.

So this was the comparison that had to begin filling the void of living out here. And no, there wasn't smugness in it. I wasn't coming back there and saying, Ah, you poor miserable prisoners of the urban clutch, the rat race. Far from it! If anything, I was looking at my old haunts and old friends with admiration. They led productive lives, for the most, and appeared refueled by them.

But those lives were simply not mine. That was the humility that must finally come: I clearly wasn't the man for that frenetic world, because, perhaps like an alcoholic, I couldn't handle the temptation of it, the stoking of ego desires that would too often pull me away from my center. Not for a moment did I believe that the bucolic lifestyle was the ultimate salvation for most people. It wasn't back to the land or else. Far from it! My friends who lived in the urban milieu could be happy there because they had obviously developed enough detachment to be able to integrate the stimulation without letting it destroy them. But, for reasons beyond my control—because of the unique mix constituting me—from boyhood on, I'd felt an innate need to complete myself in a connection with Nature, rather than in the affairs of men. Much as I might have wanted to have the corporate personality, or be a team player, the shoe never quite fit. Against its chafing, I found loosed in me a competitive aggression that I always sensed was destructive to my spirit, and offering me only restless unattainment. The money prize never seemed worth the demands of the game. Perhaps it was like what the young man said after his first long-awaited sex: "Gosh, is that all it was!" So in the end, I'd had to seek my treasures elsewhere.

Once I drove a friend of Tom's across the endless rolling hills of the Wyoming ranch. He was a city kid, fresh from the games and the gabbering peer groups. He got out of the truck to open a wire gate; suddenly his eyes widened and he breathed: "It's so...so quiet! How do you stand this quiet?" Then, someplace a coyote started to howl and the kid heard it for the first time, almost with a shudder.

And in Arizona, a young woman from Manhattan drove from the Tucson airport to the ranch, a trip that took about an hour. Yet, when she got out of her car, she was ashen. "This!" she cried, and flung her arms at the expanse of the desert and wrinkled mountains, "why, it's too much; there's something missing. It's like a toilet without any water in it!" She'd had to gulp a couple of valiums en route, just to get there at all.

In Manhattan, no, you didn't see the sky much, and every canyoned block you stared down had a concrete end to it. Out here, it was the infinity that terrified.

I realized this when, years before, I'd created a television series about the Old West (as it really was, I hoped). I spent a lot of time preparing a manual for the writers of successive episodes. Basing the series on pioneer journals from western Wyoming, and in some degree my own interviews with oldtimers, I tried to entice the writers away from the pulp-fiction fisticuffs-gunplay violence, and to lead them into a more honest portrayal, one that would show the inner violence the West wreaks on a man or woman—mainly, the agonizing abandonment that the pioneers clearly felt in those days, and, despite TV, that I still often felt now. Not only did fear from without lurk in that loneliness, but there also smoldered the age-old angers of cabin fever. In the blizzards or the privations, when these rages boiled, people exploded to kill one another. The cliché saloon-fights or arguments over cattle that city writers loved to dramatize—yes, undoubtedly some murders did spring from such macho confrontations. But early journals seemed to indicate that the pioneers' greatest struggle was simply against loneliness.

But they'd learned ways of surmounting it, at least old Clance had. He was a grizzled cowboy whom I had the pleasure to know. By the time we'd crossed paths, Clance was like a little broken bird, still flapping around with all the cricks from broncs and the aches, coughs, and scars of his decades on the lonely trail. One day Clance up and married an ugly little waif who'd been an itinerant hay cook. He brought her out to his raunchy cow camp, which had neither power nor phone, and was snowed in from November to May.

When I visited Clance at his log cabin the following spring, he was sitting in the kitchen amidst a stack of unwashed dishes, and smoking homemade cigarettes. "Yas, goddammit," he grunted, "that there woman done quit me. Said she didn't like being stuck way back here. Hell, I told her"—he flung his arm at the window—"all she had to do was set right there and watch the cars, didn't she? Now's they got the Forty Rod cutoff plowed, they's cars always goin' by—three, four a day, anyhow."

I was thinking about old Clance one afternoon when I'd gone up to fish an isolated stream in a lodgepole jungle not far from where he'd lived. To reach the stream, I had to walk several miles through dark, abandoned glades. To my surprise, I came on the moldered skeleton of an old cabin. No doubt Clance knew it was there. Probably some hunter or trapper had built it, or even a tie hack around the turn of the century when they were still cutting logs and floating them down to the Union Pacific main line. Anyhow, the builder's footsteps were gone, just like Clance's. All that remained of his life was a few old rusted cans and a scatter of square, handmade nails.

When I finally arrived at the stream, I found a deep, beautiful pool, shadowed by a high cliff. I was tired after the walk, so I sat down on a gravel bar and began to fuss with finding the right fly. It was a drowsy sort of time; I lay back against a rock and stared at the sky, which echoed with a strange, out-of-place sound—a long dull roar. As it came closer, it merged into the feathering contrail of a jet. Rarely did I see many, because no airways crossed here. But, in the crystalline air, I could identify the jet as a 727; undoubtedly some United pilot, or whoever, vectored over this shorter route to someplace.

For a moment, I could envision those passengers up in the cabin, the plugs of Muzak in their ears and their newspapers spread on cocktail trays. They'd be reading about the president negotiating this or that; and, there would surely be fighting in the Middle East, the Dow rising or falling, the Yankees winning and the Cubs losing...

So what else *was* new, really? Yes, these busy, hurrying people, fleeting across the sky at five hundred fifty knots, did have all the stimulations of modern life buzzing in their heads. But were they gaining more, growing more in those experiences than I was, an insignificant speck, sitting in the rocks beside a trout stream?

I didn't know the answer, except that I had no desire to be up in that jet, hurrying on to some importance. Indeed, perhaps that *was* the answer: that no man can travel another's path, that each must seek his own unfolding in his own unique way.

So, simply, I fished: tossed out a grasshopper fly and let it float slowly through the deep hole along the shadowed cliff. Kerr-whop! In a shower of spray and a massive slap of tail, a trout exploded in a strike, his body as brilliant as flung gold coins. He was a cutthroat, the Wyoming native species, but unlike the others I'd often caught in this stream, he was a monster of at least four pounds. The way he raced and plunged across the big pool made it obvious that he owned this space. He'd driven out all the lesser fish.

As I played him and watched his noble fight, I began to understand my own struggle, in him. Now, it's obvious that when you have a big fish on your line, you don't go woolgathering off into philosophy. Yet, as I reflected on that fish later, I could indeed see truths in him that had been gnawing at me, in my effort to fill my void of loneliness.

Clearly, this particular trout, a giant in his domain, was unequal. Why? Because nature was unequal, cruelly so, and had never pretended anything else. Clance and the other hard-handed men in their lonely cabins knew that. They had lived with nature's truth all their lives.

But me? No, I hadn't been trained to think that way. Somewhere back in the centuries, my gene pool had been persuaded to believe that science could scalpel out of it any connection with my spirit level, the "not by bread alone" part of me. Science said this was superstition, and in its place had offered me other guidance, promising to liberate me by legislating me free and equal. In dimly remembered history, from the guillotine of the French Revolution, the thunders of the Declaration of Independence and finally to the caveats of the United Nations, I was led to accept such "equality," even though nature never did.

But there was only one major problem. This equality that had been forced on me could not fill the void that my spirit felt. I wasn't alone in this "missingness." Even back in the eighteenth century, a Scottish physician began observing a strange new sickness in the world: patients who were unhappy, not really ill, but simply hurting from a vague inner malaise. "The English Malady," the doctor called it, and wrote the first textbook definition of a neurotic.

So, yes, I, like them, did hurt, and the more we multiplied into the present day, the more we fled to couches of healers who insisted we were only unhappy because we'd buried our subconscious drives of sex and aggression. But even after we'd learned to release those drives, admit them into life, there still seemed to be more and more of us—Thoreau noted this—clanking along in chain gangs of quiet desperation, feeling lost, missing something.

Our problem, then, we were told, was that we had become split men. We preached brotherly love, yet what we lived was dog-eat-dog competition. We yearned for the things in the advertisements, but never got enough of them. We were told we were free, until we tried to be. Our spirit, however faintly, was still telling us to be an individual, to cling to and preserve our tiny domain of self, just as the trout had. But if we were all *equal,* equal meant the same. And the same meant finally clinging to our credit card, because if we didn't the computer would pop us out and away: occupant, Nowhere Man.

Therefore, in our equal sameness, all that was really left for us was to cling tighter and tighter to the other togethers, talking louder, busying, hurrying as if the sheer noise of the words words words would drown our loneliness away.

So I, alone with my fish, yes, my culture would indeed consider me as an escaper, certainly counterproductive and even a threat to all others who clung together. How dared I consider myself unequal enough to want to be alone and thus have no need of the other? Didn't that smack of elitism, or even madness?

But in the eyeless windows of that old moldered log cabin, or in the memory of Clance staring out of his, I had seen unequal men. They could look without fear up to the altars of granite where the lightning is Armageddon, and the swirling white-outs of snow howl away the pretensions of lesser beings. For Clance and the rest of them had lived through the winter kills and seen the mountain daisies in the skulls of spring. Thus connected to the cycles of nature, they needed no other human company or human direction. They knew their place in the center of the All, and in this they had found not only their unique, unequal meaning, but their sacred value in the unfolding of life.

God? Did they speak of God? Probably not. They simply *heard* Him, in the silence of themselves.

And me? I wondered, when I'd finally drawn that massive, unequal cutthroat up on the rocks. He was limp; he'd given his best fight. My instinct was to grab him, seize my prize in a world that paid off only on the prize. I could brag about him that night to the people on the ranch. Photograph him so that he would become just another fish, lined up with the other fish, the triumphs that would fill our talk, because we had only to talk so as not to hear our inner silence.

When I looked at the cutthroat, his amber eye gleamed at me, as if he were reading my thoughts. I reached out to touch him, but he wouldn't be touched. With a whip of his powerful jaw he snapped my leader and flung himself back into the stream. I pawed after him, groveled in the shallows, pulling up only handfuls of mud. "God!" I shouted, that reflex curse at myself, my disbelief, and mostly at my sin of losing. The canyon walls echoed back: God! God! God!

I stood there on the rocks and had to smile. Yes, I might have been alone out here, but somehow, not nearly as lonely.

And finally, perhaps, the greatest leap was to accept my smallness.

Not the physical side of it, the being dwarfed by the sheer vastness. Undoubtedly, that did play a part in the transformation. I had only to cringe from lightning in the mountains, or to fight my way through a blizzard to see how tiny and powerless I was out here.

Perhaps it was exactly that absence of power that was the real anguish in accepting my new smallness, brought on by leaving my older values behind.

I'd never thought about it much until a delightful woman came to visit us in Arizona. She wanted a few days of winter sun, and because she lived alone in a small New England town, we felt she wouldn't suffer undue culture shock when she entered our dilatory, monastic regimen. She was certainly no "in-person," rushing frantically to the importances and urgencies of big-city business. She was contemplative, like us, one of those guests who delight me because they're self-feeders. They bring their books and knitting and are not always badgering me to saddle up horses that might buck them off, or take them hunting for quail they usually can't hit, and then sulk. No, this lovely lady seemed content merely to join Teddy's routine, which consisted of milking the cow in the morning, collecting the eggs, and feeding the chickens. Then, without apologies, we could all return to our typewriters or our reading.

But when I'd finished my morning's work, and came over to Teddy's office, a curious scene was in progress. Often, Teddy would spend the morning totting up the ranch books, or editing my books or those of others. She'd always be busy right up to the moment of sitting down for lunch. But when I poured sherry for all of us, Teddy and our friend were locked in such an intense discussion that neither picked up her glass.

"The point is, my dear," the New England lady was saying, "milking your cow, getting your eggs, that's all very fine, of course; it's pleasant for you. But with your background, your education—with so much to be *done* in the world—it's simply not enough."

I frowned. "What's not enough?"

"Our lives," Teddy said, and smiled.

I was astounded that she could smile, because I certainly didn't feel like it. As I listened, quite incredulous, our friend, with the best intentions no doubt, was lecturing Teddy on the code of the Performance Ethic: what was *expected* of us, the favored few blessed by good family and education, and chosen to become the leaders of our society. How *dared* people of our backgrounds content themselves out playing with milk cows, chipmunks, or whatever? There was so much that needed to be *done.*

As our guest continued, by now broadening her "lesson" to include me, I felt that she was simply giving a reprise of the old culture lie of sense of worth: that we be judged on what we do, not on what we are. Yet there was clearly another ingredient here, another "oughtness" which demanded us to save the world. We must.

Indeed, I thought, if I could convince myself that I had no spiritual side of me, no not-by-bread-alone part of my nature, then I would only have to accept the popular conception that I was my own god. If I didn't save the world, who would?

I was reminded then of what one reviewer had written about my earlier book about coming to Wyoming, *New Lease on Life.* It was fine, he said, for me to run off to a ranch and fight lonely little battles out in the sagebrush. But didn't I realize that the real fight lay in the ghettos of the cities, in the courage of the freedom fighters, and those young men and women rising on the barricades to protest the senseless killing in Vietnam? The only fight now was against poverty, injustice, racism. What needed to be done in the world was political action, confrontation that would force a change in man.

I thought for a moment of our son John, sitting in his room one night at Stanford when a group of student revolutionaries, most of them his good friends, burst in on him. They begged him to join their sacking of the administration building. When he protested that he had too much studying to do, and a track meet the next day, they cried: "That's simply not enough. That's not what we're here for!"

What *are* we here for? I wondered then. Was it better for John to go with them and watch them set fire to the administration building and heave IBM typewriters out the windows? Was it better for him to go with them and cut cane for Castro in Cuba, or simply to go to the ranch in Wyoming and cut hay? Would either action have saved more lives from the senseless killing?

I suppose I used to think it did. In my old city existence, when I had the feeling of power and proximity to the problems of the day, I wrote many thousands of words, pushing my ideas for saving the world. Now, however, in the shadow of Tolstoy, changing humanity seemed far less important than changing ourselves.

Indeed, that's why we were here, and why Teddy could answer our kindly old friend with no more than a smile.

"Either I marry him, señora, or I will spend the rest of my life with a broken heart."

In the sunlit Arizona kitchen of Maude and all the rest of our "ladies," Refugia was clutching Teddy to her. Everyone had wet eyes. It was hard to believe that this loyal, wonderful girl whom we had smuggled into our hearts, and who had lived with us for five years, was finally leaving.

We'd seen it coming, of course. Refugia had blossomed into a beautiful Mexican woman, with traces of the classic serenity of her Pima Indian forebears. Though we'd arranged for her legal immigration to the U.S., we never expected her to stay with us forever. Indeed, we wanted to help her attain *la vida mejor* ("the better life"), of which she'd always dreamed, from the time she'd been a little girl in a Sonora adobe with a dirt floor.

We'd tried to interest her in a succession of eligible swains, everything from wetbacks to Border Patrolmen to young itinerant cowboys. Ironically, Refugia's most ardent suitor was an ambitious young Mexican who not only had U.S. papers but held a high-paying job in construction. By visit and long-distance calls, he pleaded his troth desperately, to which Refugia could only sniff: "He's too Indian for me!" He was a Tarahumara.

No, the only man for her proved to be a nonpapered Mexican boy named Jesus, or Chuy for short. Actually, he was quite short, held no job, and apparently had a resounding temper. Chuy was definitely not our choice, but then again, beloved Refugia was not our daughter. She was a grown woman: she knew what she wanted, and after the final weep-out—Chuy or a broken heart—a date was set. We would give Refugia her wedding in the little Sasabe church, followed by a *gran baile* and reception at our ranch house.

I tried to absent myself from the preparation phase, but escape was impossible. The house throbbed as Teddy and phalanxes of sturdy Mexican women hurled themselves into a sentimental orgy. An old family wedding dress was tucked up and around Refugia's lovely bosom. Pre-dieu kneelers for the bride and groom were decorated in sprays of flowers which busy Mexican fingers had fashioned out of pink Kleenex. A fatted calf was killed (obviously one of ours; I never wanted to ask). Old Mexican men who knew how to *barbacoa*—barbecue Sasabe-style in galvanized garbage cans—kept digging a pit behind the ranch house, stoking the coals of mesquite. It was only *after* the wedding that a horrified county agent told me: never barbecue anything in galvanized metal, stomach cancer and who knows what else.

Anyhow, we had enough else to keep us busy. From Refugia's home down in Sonora and from passing wetbacks, we learned that Refugia's family had forbidden the wedding. Undoubtedly, we thought, it was just natural familial reluctance. Refugia's many brothers didn't like Chuy. They'd get over it. After all, the Pima Indians had always been peaceful.

On the wedding afternoon, pickups and a few old junker cars carrying Refugia and Chuy's family and friends crossed the border and met us at an unused Sasabe, Arizona, church. With no heat in the little church, it was one cold adobe; but who cared. Teddy wept joyously as I marched the bride away to the sound of Lohengrin on a tape recorder that failed to start on cue. Everyone knelt amidst pink Kleenex, and used the rest of it to dab eyes. A hearty Franciscan in his brown robes, a veteran of Indian missions, gave the blessing and the deed was done.

Then we returned en masse to the ranch, ready for feasting on galvanized *barbacoa* and dancing the night away to the tunes of Peter's country-western band. Because the boys played on the border circuit, they did a lot of Mexican songs. We let the tequila flow and danced to "Rancho Grande," "Malaguena," and "La Burrita."

We even had a dance that the groom, Chuy, suggested:
the "Baile Verde." In this Mexican custom, when mem-
bers of the wedding party cut in on the bride and groom,
they pin green money on them. Refugia and Chuy were
beaming in the fluttering bills just when another Bill
tapped me on the shoulder and said, "You better come
outside."

This was none other than Bill Kent, Teddy's brother
who had smuggled Refugia to Mexico five years earlier.
Now, returning from Latin America to visit us, it
appeared that his first Refugia mission had definitely been
simpler!

What confronted me in the shadows of the back door
were three young Mexicans. They were unshaven, faces
smeared with blood, and one of them was brandishing an
empty tequila bottle. "Hermana," he slurred, and swayed
into me. "Hermana." Only then did I recognize that two
of these smarmy, surly types were Refugia's brothers,
including one who had spent time in the U.S. "casa" for
drug-running. The other Mexican was simply a comrade
in arms, and impossibly drunk. Still, I'd known Refugia's
brothers for years and liked them. They were decent,
hard-working kids, until this moment when the tequila or
the Mexican feud-blood had flushed up their high cheek-
bones and made their eyes gleaming black and mean.

They demanded to dance with their sister. Well, I tried
to avoid it, gave them perfectly good reasons that this was
mi casa, they wouldn't want me coming to *their casa
borracho* and on the fight, would they? So why ruin a good
party? Forget bothering their sister. We'd feed them and
give them a place to sleep for the night.

"Hermana," they kept breathing, until finally I shrugged
and said, Oh, hell, go in and give her a kiss then, and be on
your way.

What happened thereafter was unclear but utterly
predictable. In the midst of Pete's band tinking "Baile

Verde," either Chuy slugged the ex-con brother or vice versa. Doesn't matter. The entire happy porch disintegrated into a howling fistfight, the band still playing on. When poor Refugia interceded between Chuy and her brothers, Chuy accused her of "not siding with his blood," and flung her across the porch into a glass door. As friends and families began punching it out, there were screams of fleeing Mexican children, somebody fell into the drums, and through it all, our little granddaughter, Tess, lay asleep on the living room sofa.

By now, our own shock troops had been stunned into action. Peter took off his guitar and with marine Bill and a big bass player, managed to get the brawling brothers and their amigo out to the back door. Here, the oldest brother swore an oath that he would kill the groom. That's what he'd come for. And I was counterthreatening that we'd call the Border Patrol. Please, amigos, behave, just go down to the arroyo and sleep it off. But the sacred honor of the family was at stake, kill the outsider. There was more punching and shoving between us. Finally, as the "Skipper" of this desperate rear-guard action, I had no choice but to take Bill and Peter's advice. With their assistance, we heaped, unfortunately quite roughly, all the rubber-legged avengers into the back of our pickup, locked its camper shell, and hero Bill thundered down the road with clear instructions to dump them across the border in Mexico.

No sooner had I reentered the house, thinking that's that and wiping my hands clean, than the telephone rang. Sheriff's office. It had a report from a terrified young Mexican who said he'd given a hitchhike to three men on the Sasabe road. After attacking him with a twelve-inch knife, they'd also told him before he escaped that they were en route to the Carney ranch to kill someone else. "Just thought I'd warn you, Mr. Carney," said the sheriff.

"Oh, that's all right," I answered confidently, explaining how we'd already taken care of the three fellows and dumped them across the line into Mexico.

"Yes, but," the sheriff said, "it's only twenty miles or so."

"What's that got to do with it?"

"Mr. Carney," his voice had a wry and tired practicality, "from what I know of people like these, they'll be back. Take my word, you can count on it." Then he added apologetically that he didn't have a car he could send me. Perhaps I ought to try the Border Patrol.

Or the Mounties, or whomever. Because just at that moment in walked Bill, grinning with a beer in his hand.

"You got them," I echoed, "to Mexico so quick?"

"Ah, hell, Big O. They promised me they were going to behave and hitch north now. I just dumped them there by the ranch fence, a couple of miles from here."

Before I could even groan, two little Mexican girls, relatives of somebody's were tugging at my coat. They led me into our bedroom where Teddy and Refugia were both sobbing, with the hearty Franciscan patting their back. In briefest summary: the groom had exploded in fury against the bride, and not only had managed to punch out Refugia, but also had attacked his own protesting mother. She had literally flown onto his back like a little flapping bird, crying, "Con amor, con amor!" He had flung her over a chair. He also kicked the priest in the privates before the priest finally punched him and knocked him down.

Sic transit marriage, which lasted approximately two hours.

Refugia was moaning, "Nunca, nunca!" Never would she be married to this man, and, yes, señor and señora had been right all along. This was a horrible mistake. He was the wrong man; she would never see him again. So get rid of him, please; get rid of everyone, and we would lock Refugia in her room where he couldn't come and hurt her. As our mournful procession led her through the house to her own quarters, Refugia's tears were now spilling down over the happy "Baile Verde" dollars still pinned to her wedding dress. Hero Bill nudged me with his beer and said: "What do we do now? Ask for our money back?"

No, what we did then was for Teddy, the priest, and I to assume the wrecking job of telling the groom that the marriage was over, *termino.* Though the Franciscan speaks fluent enough Spanish to give sermons in it, and I can even write it passably, by default we evolved that Teddy, in her gruesome kitchen Spanish, would deliver our exteme unction to poor Chuy. She was our most sympathetic voice, we felt, and thus the priest and I sat in mute cowardice while she described the proposed annulment.

"No," Chuy said in a low voice. Then it grew higher, "No, no!" and louder until his "nuncas" went screaming through the house, with the priest and I pursuing him because he was now assaulting the sanctuary of Refugia's room, tearing off the window screen and trying to crawl in after her. When that didn't work, and after much entreating and sobbing, he finally succeeded in getting through the door and when last seen was dragging Refugia like a sack of flour down the driveway.

At that point I'd reached my pain-in-the-neck threshold. I'd had one fistfight already with the brothers. My last, before that, had been at Pensacola, I think, in 1942. So I'm not exactly Jake LaMotta or noted for being a defensive lineman. Nonetheless, I felt no choice but to make a flying tackle of young Señor Chuy and ended up beating his head in the rocks of the driveway. This was a curious fight in chronological terms. Every time Chuy would cry "uncle" (it was probably *tio* if I was hearing his language correctly, which I doubt), then I would release him on his promise that he would behave himself and go home someplace, wherever home was, until poor Refugia had a chance to catch her breath. Yet, the moment after Chuy seemed to surrender, he'd lash out again toward her room and begin tearing down doors and screens. Once he took a punch at Teddy, who was now pleading with him. To avenge that dastardly act, I shot out a six-inch right hand, filled with such massive power that it not only missed completely but spun me onto my back into a camellia plant where I was impaled and kicking like a turtle. Meanwhile, the priest had caught it again in the groin, Teddy was beating tiny fists on Chuy's back, and, finally, my lassitudinous shock troops chose to join the fray. Peter simply took Chuy's arm and twisted it behind him in a half nelson, to which Pete added a finger twist of uncertain origin, the end result being that he screwed Chuy down into the driveway, howling in pain. From there, we bundled him into our car for a special-delivery trip to the bus station in Tucson. There was surely no bus at 2 A.M., but since the pink Kleenex and dollar bills still hung on him, we didn't mind asking him to wait.

However, his captors, Bill and Peter, again got a short way down the road and decided, who needs the trip in the middle of the night? Certainly they didn't. So they compromised by driving Chuy four miles away, to where our Mexican cowboy lives. This gallant gentleman popped Chuy into his big double bed, where he could sleep right beside him for the rest of the awful night.

It was nearly 1 A.M. when we regrouped in the ranch kitchen. Mortified Mexican relatives were diligently mopping up the wet Kleenex flowers and shattered glass. We were all so "strung out," as the boys in the band called it, so keyed, that we couldn't possibly go to bed. We simply sat there, mourning the ludicrous mess, and congratulating ourselves on how neatly we finally handled it. Teddy and the priest had already collected many signatures on the annulment paper, testifying that the marriage had not been consummated. The belligerent groom was safely incarcerated four miles away where the Mexican avengers could never find him. And they, undoubtedly, had lived up to their promise and begun a contrite hitchhike north.

We had barely chuckled about it before the back door banged open. In lurched two of the brothers, the new blood from our last fight now crusted in with the old scars. Their amigo had passed out somewhere in the mesquite, another brooding assailant to contend with when he sobered up in the morning. And now the brothers added a second oath of vengeance. The groom would doubly die because he not only had offended them, but had taken a punch at me. The Mexicans call shame *verguenza*, and there was a steam of it exuding from the brothers. Any reasoning with them was superfluous. Death must come: if it took years they'd find Chuy and kill him. Yet there Chuy was, four miles away. As certain as the sunrise, next morning he'd be up and running for Refugia's room. So we could look forward to a sunlit knife fight, or guns, or God knew what.

Our pleading with them led to shoving, so my third fistfight of the evening erupted. But unfortunately by then, we were all down to glancing blows and love taps. Peter interceded by putting his arms around Refugia's brothers, and took them to his adobe to patch their wounds. In the morning, after a short, restless night, we had a peace treaty of sorts, and the brothers grumbled back down the mesquite trail to Mexico, where they'd lie in wait for Chuy, if he ever dared return.

By this time, my foreman had smuggled Chuy onto a friendly Greyhound bus, and off he went to somewhere that I hoped I'd never find. Goodbye, good riddance, and Refugia, our annulled Juliet, would be back with us again.

That night, the telephone began to ring, again the next morning and the following afternoon. Chuy from a paybooth somewhere. Within two days, Refugia had forgiven him. In a week she was gone, for the last time, happily married and living in a green pasture far from us, and, we hoped, far from the vengeance of the brothers.

A love story in the desert, ended now, not only for Refugia, but, as it turned out, for all of us.

On an afternoon not long thereafter, Teddy and I were sitting in a bleak, empty California ranch house, a totally strange place that gave me the feeling that I was somehow in the stage set of a bad play. I knew the cast, of course, because Peter and Rita were there with us, also John and Nancy, our family architects. And Tom was at the other end of the telephone in New York, eagerly awaiting our decision.

The choice was clear-cut now. We'd located what appeared to be an excellent ranch in the mountains of central California. Within the next few hours, we'd have to decide whether to negotiate on it or to abandon the idea, and remain on the Las Delicias.

As we pondered and argued, a coastal storm swept in. First came wind, whistling through the old house which had evolved out of a log cabin, built in the 1850s. Rain began drumming the tin roof and weeping down windows which had neither shades nor curtains, and were all different sizes so that none of the frames fit properly. Because Teddy and I were seated on the only chairs, the rest of the family was reduced to pacing the floor between us. Even that was an effort. The floor slanted so badly that John resembled a sea captain on the deck of a sinking ship.

"This dump!" he cried. "To trade off the Las Delicias, those beautiful adobes you've worked on so much." He shook his head. "Even to consider this, you've both got to be out of your minds!"

"Yes, probably we are," I said, and then, as if to

reconvince myself, I began spooling off the practical considerations that had led us to this point. Of course, John and Tom both, from their years on the Las Delicias, knew much of the problem. For all our love of the place, it was still a desert ranch. In the eleven years we had it, only two or three summers had adequate rains. In this particular cycle of drought, the burroweed and mesquite had infested the ranges so heavily that for all our conservation efforts, we doubted if we could ever reverse the trend. Even our neighbors, who could afford massive brush-clearing programs at fifty dollars an acre, seemed to be fighting a losing battle. When I asked one of them what he intended to do about the new shoots of mesquite growing up in his grassland, he simply shook his head: "Leave 'em for the next man."

We, too, were doing the same thing, and with great sadness. The summers had been so dry that even the Sonoran masked bobwhite had been unable to reproduce. The Fish and Wildlife Service finally had to move our hopeful program to a higher-altitude ranch with more moisture.

No feed for our cattle, and a changing world: that was my summary to John. The booming growth of Tucson was spreading out to jeopardize all the ranches in massive Pima County. This was critical because we owned only a small proportion of the land on the Las Delicias. The vast majority was leased from the state—actually, only fifteen percent of Arizona's landmass was in private hands. When the state owned land, this meant that people from nearby Tucson would demand increasing access to it, which was their right under law. We could look forward to more hunters, woodcutters, sunbunnies with campers and motorbikes, and just plain vandals. It's hard to run a ranch on public property. Then too, taxes were rising rapidly, and water was so short it was just a matter of time before people would take it instead of the cows.

Once we'd reached this sad realization, we'd begun actively searching for a ranch that would have a solid block of deeded land, no government leases, in an area of stronger, more predictable grass. By owning every acre of it, we could develop it as we wanted into a ranch that would be less nerve-racking than one in the desert. Not only did Peter and Rita want to sink their teeth into a place like that, but now, too, they had to think about reasonable accessibility to schools for Tess and Joe. The Las Delicias was nearly an hour and a half from school on the schoolbus, and twice that when the kids reached high school.

Thus, when we'd driven up a long valley in California, studded by oak trees, and the tall grass grazed by deer, Pete had smiled and said: "This is the one, Big O."

I'd seen enough ranches in my life to know that he was right. Here in this basin of mountains lay our protection and promise for the future.

"But it's the human cost," John kept insisting, "the sheer effort of you and Fred having to begin all over again." Though he and Tom now lived in cities, they'd spent enough years out bucking hay bales or chasing cattle to know that ranching was far from the idyll you might see on "Dallas." To make the California ranch even livable, we'd have to build a house. Of course, John and Nancy were eager to design it, but he warned, "You've got to realize, Big O, building way back here is going to cost a bundle." Water would have to piped to the site, and even Pete was admitting that more water would be needed if we hoped to scatter our cows up into the hills, so that we could run enough to make the place pay. So we were looking at pipelines, road repairs, bridges, old barns that had to be torn down—cleaning up the junk and mistakes of a hundred years, until it was our junk and our mistakes, begun again.

"But you've got to admit, John," I said as he paced the sagging old house, "this is a beautiful piece of land."

"They're all beautiful. Wyoming, Arizona. But what for?"

"For us," Teddy answered.

John whirled to me. "Come on, Big O. Be honest. You've always been restless out on these ranches. All the problems, nothing going right. What makes you think this is going to be any different?"

"Because maybe I'm different, John. Or at least," I added with a smile, "older."

"That's the point, don't you see?" John's voice began to tighten. "You're fifty-nine, Big O, Fred is fifty-four. For the twenty years you've been living out on these ranches, your career as a writer has obviously been suffering. Well, who needs it? You've got a last chance now to cut with it, yes, give it up. Let Pete stay on a ranch if he wants, but you, with the years you've got left, take them and move to some comfortable, civilized place where you can enjoy them."

"But, John," Teddy said, "we enjoy this. This *is* what we are."

An hour or so later, the low clouds had lifted and I walked with John through the mud out to a sagging old barn. "Big O," John said, "I certainly didn't mean to shake you and Fred up so much. I hope you realize I was only trying to play devil's advocate for both of you."

"I know that, John. And we can sure use one."

Then we stood together beside Peter, who was studying the old leaking barn and deciding how he could take it down. I could only think of the time when Teddy and I had tried to persuade Peter to leave ranching. There was no future in it, we told him. What he or any young man needed was to go into a company—manufacturing, real estate, tractors, whatever interested him—work his way up.

"Company!" he'd cried. "I know your companies and your friends who run 'em. They work a man from nine to five and when he goes home he's done with all the hassles of it. If you fire him, so what? He walks across the street and gets another job. But on this land, living with these animals and busting your guts to keep 'em alive, this isn't a job. This is life. You can't just fire a man from his life!"

Or, as Crazy Horse had said more than a hundred years before: "You cannot sell the land on which the people walk."

Later, in silence, Teddy and I went high up on one of the grassy hills and sat under a dripping live oak. Well, what more to say? Were we making this move because of my restlessness? Or was it because I'd finally grown beyond it? When we were young, we could make such rash choices, as perhaps we'd done when we left Beverly Hills. Then we had the time and energy left to get away with them. But now, edging toward the final quadrant of our lives, we had less of those precious commodities.

So why not give up the idea? Move to an easy little house on a beach someplace. Write my books no longer in the hard loneliness of the land, but in the comfortable company of my peers, golfing off into the sunset. Obviously it made sense. It was even tempting. In the new "social life" it seemed to offer, I could envision all sorts of stimuli pumping into my aging brain: conversation with fascinating people, new contacts opening up undreamed-of horizons. After all, as I'd been told so long before, the people who read books live mainly in urban communities. They were my audience, and just down the beach from some mythical retirement community lay the film studios, with the telephones that still might ring. So, get off the range, that's what John was saying, get back into real life.

And speaking of backs, of course, the back was where the aching was, the familiar yearning for stroking. Real life could provide that. And much of the restlessness of the writer was simply his longing for affirmation. As novelist Ernest Gann had put it: a writer is the world's most unneeded human. Daily he has to persuade himself that the book he slaves over for a year or so is going to be worth more to somebody than, say, a bottle of Scotch at the same price.

In addition, by the very nature of his trade, a writer must have a built-in sense of incompletion. It's the curse of any artist: you see a dream out there, but regardless of how hard you work to bring it to reality, the end product never quite satisfies, never matches the original inspiration.

And in my case at least, this gap was widened by a lack of talent. Oh, I could put words down all right, and I enjoyed it. But when I'd see the real writers up there, blessed with such powers of illusion, intellectual depth, and steeped in the classics, I could only be appalled at the shabby tools I brought to my task. I'm not an intellectual. I prefer baseball to Bach and quail to quatrains. As for the celebrity "literati" of the writer's conferences and the New York cocktail party circuit, I find the majority boring popinjays, and anyway would rather be out fishing.

So what then? Run on, ever searching, uncompleted? Or root in finally and accept?

For a moment, the years of learning, of trying to change, filmed in front of my eyes. Yes, there had been progress, slight as it may have seemed. The committing and the recommitting had done strange things. Perhaps it had been the waiting without hope that was slowly healing the two sides of me into one new man. In the real-life world, where growth was measured by dollar signs, the ranches did manage to limp along now. And to my typewriter had come other interventions of providence. For instance, a novel about Mexico I'd written ten years before—which had been rejected all over New York—now suddenly seemed to have found its time, and was coming out not only as a book but perhaps as a film. There would be other films, too, and even journalism after all these years: more ideas than I seemed to have time to write.

And a different sense of time too, because not only was Peter removing much of the ranching responsibility from me, but also we were seeing, in his children, and then John and Nancy's Nora, the family rejoin as an expanded unit, the same old cottage industry begun so long ago now bringing us delicious nights of babysitting, and tea parties with the girls and little Joe, out on the back porch of wherever we would finally call home.

The dream was that all of this would be coming here with us to California. But in a final spasm of doubt, I still had to glance at Teddy, sitting next to me under the oak. "We could, you know, sell off the majority of the Las Delicias land and keep a few hundred acres around the headquarters. It would be stretching us, but it would begin to pay for this place, and at the same time, you and I could still live in the desert. That would mean we wouldn't have to build anything here. You wouldn't have to go through the orgy of moving again. We could just stay down there and let the kids fend for themselves."

"You mean, stay in our retirement home?"

"Well, we could keep a couple of horses."

"That," she answered, "would be like going to a dance and not dancing. Of course I don't want to leave Arizona. How could I, that awful uprooting? And besides, I love the desert. But to stay there when it's not right, when it means cutting off from the kids, I couldn't do that, darling, and I doubt if you could either. In Peter's favorite phrase," she smiled, "how rash he can be! We have to go for it!"

"That's what you really want?"

"I know it's God's will. It's where we've been heading all these years."

"I hope," I said, and hugged her.

As an old rancher once told me: "Son, when you get your neck stuck out in this business, you can almost bet on two things gonna happen. First, they break the cattle market on you, and then God decides to have it quit rainin'."

What the rancher neglected to mention was the third nightmare: interest rates soaring to record highs. In the sudden crunching of recession, a delightful desert ranch in Arizona was the last thing any buyer would ever want. "You know," said a real estate broker, "nobody really *needs* a ranch. You may be in for quite a wait, trying to dump this one."

The only problem was, we couldn't wait.

On the afternoon of decision in California, that was the gamble I knew I was making. The owner of the California ranch, himself financially stretched in the recession, had eventually agreed that he would trade me his ranch for the Las Delicias and other emoluments. Now this was a perfectly legal tax deal, he and I both avoiding payment of capital gains on our respective properties. In fact, the Internal Revenue code had been altered to favor exchanges of this type. But the hidden wrinkle was that the California owner wanted only cash out of his ranch. He had no interest whatsoever in the Las Delicias. Therefore, acting as his agent, I agreed to sell the Las Delicias for him, and guarantee him his total cash payment within eighteen months.

The transaction was so complex that after the lawyers had gnawed it around, the months had spooled away so that now, when Teddy and I returned from California, we had only a year remaining in which to sell the Las Delicias and complete our part of the bargain. In the meantime, because the desert was burning up in drought, we'd moved Peter, Rita, cows, horses, and truckloads of equipment over to California. We were committed indeed, and should we not be able to find a buyer for the Las Delicias, I was in the catbird seat of having to buy it back myself, thus ending up as the owner of three ranches, en route to debtor's prison!

Needless to say, during those bleak months of waiting and hoping, there was not a great deal of creative writing being accomplished. What my typewriter spooled out instead were brochures and ads, deals, and pleas to anyone I ever dreamed of who might be interested in a beautiful winter home in the sun.

It had seemed in our eleven years on the Las Delicias that dozens of people had told us they'd love to own that ranch. But when our distress call went out now, only a vast, echoing silence came back. As I was told again and again, why should any sane investor dump a large bundle of cash into a hole in the desert when, with absolutely no risk, he could put the same funds into the money market and draw the highest interest in history? Besides, the desert was surely a rockpile right then. In the words of our Mexican foreman, Teddy and I were "abandonados." In a house stripped of some of its furniture, with an empty range searing away in hot, dry winds, there was nobody there but us chickens: about a dozen of them who were too old to lay and too tough to eat; one old bird dog, and two crippled horses.

It was an anguishing time as Teddy and I showed the ranch to a dwindling trickle of prospects. Every canyon, every flowerbed seemed to hold a memory for us: the sweat and tears of making the desert home. As I'd drive some potential buyer and wife out across miles of burroweed, I'd find myself telling them about old Red and the cattle drive, or where the rattler had nearly gotten Teddy in the barn. Too many memories, I'm sure, and often the wrong ones for good salesmanship. But even as sorry as this land looked now, the old lore and old roots were deep within us, and we could hope that somebody might buy it who could love it as we did.

Among the lookers who came to the ranch were some curious types. The most hopeless were flinty-eyed folk from a tract house or a bleak forty-acre farm. They'd use such phrases as, "Nice little spread you got here," as if it were peanut butter. Or, the wife would say: "Hun, ain't that a gorgeous Messican anteek." Actually, Teddy would answer, it's French. Oh. Then we'd take them out to the adobe barn where they'd kick the tire of our tractor to prove they knew it was soft. Or, in the mesquite corral, the wife would jab her hand at my stud colt, Baboquivari, approaching him from his blind eye, and he'd be so startled he'd almost bite her. Clearly, these were people in love with the idea of having a ranch, and not having a notion how to pay for it. Probably, it was just hot in town that afternoon and they wanted a drive up into the mountains.

Other lookers were what my Mexican foreman called "multimillionarios." The American "multis" had heard about the ranch in the *Wall Street Journal.* They'd come swooping down in their private planes, and after I'd bounce them through every canyon and shadow of ancient lore, they'd begin glancing at their watches. What they wanted were numbers, cash flow, depreciation. And when I answered by showing them ancient Hohokam potsherds lying in the sand, one multi had simply shaken his head and breathed, "Are you trying to tell me that people actually lived in this god-forsaken place for thousands of years?"

Of course, it really didn't matter what I was trying to tell him. The price was too high, and the times too bad. As the months spooled away, our anxiety increased. On our nightly walks in the desert, Teddy would keep saying, "It will sell one day. I know it will. You've just got to put it in God's hands."

Well, I'd manage to for the rest of that night, but in the cold light of morning, I'd find myself leaping up like a trout at some new hope. Because now, an "instant buyer" had materialized. This shadowy gentleman drove up one afternoon, took a cursory look around, and announced, "It's a deal. I'll take it."

"Ah . . . when?"

"Have the title company draw up the papers. I'll go in and sign on Monday."

Hooray! The check is in the mail. But when, breathless, I called the title company Monday, Tuesday, again on Thursday, the shadow never appeared.

By then, in late May, with the deadline only six months away, Teddy and I were praying fervently. It was as if the Las Delicias, because we'd loved it so much, was one of our children. Into it we'd poured our hopes. We knew how good it was. And yet, out in the cold world now, the child had failed, disappointed us terribly. In addition, on the California ranch, our cattle were aborting or dying, typical of a desert herd in a strange environment. Also, Pete was stumbling onto the usual hidden surprises in a new place that always had to be papered over with money. In fact, late in May, Teddy and I went to California, hoping to put an arm into that leaky dike. When we returned to Arizona, the desert was scalding hot. Our foreman met us at the airport and he was sweating profusely. "Que noticias?" ("What news?"), I asked him.

"Ah," he shrugged, "vino un hombre. Quiere comprar el rancho."

Well, I'd heard so often that a man had come and wanted to buy the ranch that I barely had the energy to ask, What man?

My foreman answered with a familiar Mexican name. The prospect was a rancher from nearby Sonora, just below Sasabe. We'd had a lot of these good-neighbor lookers, too, and they were usually no more than that. So, almost jocosely, I asked: "Un multimillionario, el?"

My foreman gave that wonderful palms-up, shoulder shrug of Mexico. "No mas que millionario," he answered. "Y muy coyote, muy doro"—very rough, very hard to deal with—"pero quisas bastante"—but maybe enough.

I was prepared to dismiss it as another faded hope, until the following afternoon, when up drove the Mexican rancher and a phalanx of his brothers, real estate agents, and even a banker from Caborca, Sonora.

We sat out on the big porch of the Las Delicias where Refugia's brothers and Chuy had had their dreadful fight over the baile verde. I won't say we fought, the Mexican rancher and I. Sulked would be a better word. Definitely, si, he wanted the ranch. He owned many thousands of acres in Sonora, but now, with the always unpredictable political situation there, he was looking toward getting some of his *huevos* ("eggs") out of that *canasta* ("basket"), invest the pesos in the U.S.

The question: Exactly how many pesos would he come up with?

For five hours, I found myself in a skull-numbing negotiation, entirely in Spanish. Though a Mexican-American real estate broker was involved, and could translate the fine points that I would miss in the Byzantine bargaining, it soon became painfully clear that I was up against one very sharp cookie. With every jiggering or lowering of the bid, I'd be clicking out mortgage figures on my calculator—and the Mexican would always arrive at the answer ahead of me, in his head! I was astounded at his shrewdness, and mostly at his frugality. He gave me a stern warning not to remove a single light bulb from la casa. Then, the antique furniture, that of course was included?

No way, I said. *Cosas personales.*

Sulk. Finally I had to bring Teddy out onto the porch and into the trenches. In her kitchen Spanish she told him, yes, we might consider selling him separately certain pieces.

"Que costo?" His arm would fling up at a breakfront or some old Mexican bench that penitentes had probably knelt on at church. When Teddy would give him a rough price, he'd blanch. He was supposed to be buying a ranch, not a furniture store! When I finally told him that neither horses nor saddles were included in the purchase, he exploded. Mind you, here was a man who probably owned on his Mexican ranches two hundred horses and saddles. I thought the entire deal had crashed, until the wise real estate agent murmured in mendicant Spanish that he would personally buy the rancher a horse and saddle to go with the place.

Conforme ("agreed")! When they drove down the road that night, after seven vodkas, I waved the agreement paper at Teddy and said this was it! "Don't get your hopes up," she sighed. "We've been here before."

No, not exactly, and it took me ten awful days to find out why. The Mexican rancher had framed such an exotic deal that my own bank in Tucson didn't want any part of it. Neither did the California owner and his lawyers. Even my steady, long-suffering accountant said we were taking a dreadful risk, with so little cash up front and so much trust placed in the word of a Mexican.

Yet trust was all we had going for us, and I accepted the deal as the last details were finally hammered out. By then Teddy had managed to put it into God's hands, but the gamble she took was in her own. With the help of her Mexican sturdies out of Sasabe, the same loyal women who had cut up all the pink Kleenex flowers for Refugia's wedding, they and Teddy heroically stevedored us, cats, dogs, bag and baggage out of the Las Delicias—in seven days! And all this before the first hard dollar, peso, or even pony and saddle had changed hands.

Because of the complex international negotiation, I arranged a meeting at the Mountain Oyster Club in Tucson, where we would deal. This meant flying in the

California owner and his lawyer, plus our own banker, accountant, title company people, all to be joined by the legions from Mexico. A luncheon at high noon, to sign and seal the Las Delicias away.

Because the telephones below Sasabe rarely work, I had no guarantee that the Mexican rancher was really en route. Maybe they stopped him at the border; maybe the cattle trail below Sasabe was out in a flash flood. Or, he had tire trouble, the curse of Mexican driving. Whatever, noon passed into being 1 P.M., "our side" sitting at the lunch table, sipping cocktails, with the bankers and important people glancing at their watches, as if to say, Carney's done it again. Another ghost buyer evaporating into the Mexican desert.

At 1:42 the Mexican rancher came in, beaming sunnily. He gave not a word of explanation. We had to assume he was simply operating on Sonora time. Within a half hour, all the papers were signed and the Las Delicias gone. There was only one small detail. No money had yet reached the bank.

Later that afternoon I talked to my brother, Peter, who runs a mining business in Mexico and knows the Sonora game. "You're crazy to leave there under those circumstances! You'll never get paid," he said.

Well, we were crazy indeed. Because in the dusk, Teddy and I loaded the last boxes into our stationwagon and drove down the long road out of the ranch. None of Faustino's dying steers dotted the arroyos. No Border Patrol cars to pick up Refugia. No Sonoran masked bobwhite. Not even the shadows of old Red, or Cora, or Chisty, or all the birds and the beasts here, who had shared so much with us. We drove out without a tear or a look back. It could only be like that, leaving a love, and going on trust and hope from then on.

Four days later, when we were in Wyoming and I was about to take my first float down the Green River, a call

came from the bank in Tucson. Yes, the money had
arrived from Mexico. Everything was in order. The deal
had closed.

There was a sense of relief, and nostalgia too, as we
picked up again the threads of our life in Wyoming. It was
just Teddy and I, as it had been so many years before. In
the end is my beginning—or at least so I was hoping now.
And hope to a writer is the old reflex of trying to put it into
words. I felt finally that somewhere in these years of
changing, I had a tale to tell. "But I've been at this thing
so damn long," I'd say to Teddy. "All the years, all the
tries to put it down."

"Just keep trying. It'll come."

God's hands? Yes, again. Always.

Now, almost anyone ought to know that you can't write
a book when you're staring down at a trout stream. Nor
does it make a whole lot of sense to work on the same book
for so long, and, over the advice of loved ones and steely-
eyed professionals, still refuse to give it up.

But that's exactly the point I'd reached by a warm
morning in September. The Green River below my office
window was dappling with coquettish trout. Lunking
rainbows rolled up at me and leered; then some deep-
bellied brook leaped all the way out of the water so that I
couldn't possibly not see him. They knew better than I
that fall was in the air. They wouldn't have many days left
like this glorious one. Even a cow moose—I had to watch
her as she moved through the willows that had rusted up
in frost—with one cranky lunge, splashed out into the
river and left her disconsolate calf behind. Wean him
before winter, kick him out on his own.

And my own? My impossible calf, this book, was still
lying in pieces all around my typewriter, blocks of words
that I couldn't pound into any sense, scribbled ideas that

had crackled brilliant at the time and were now mostly unreadable. It made me think of T.S. Eliot, who mirrored the same frustration when he wrote:

So here I am, in the middle way, having had
     twenty years,
Twenty years largely wasted,
Trying to learn to use words, and every attempt
Is a wholly new start, and a different kind of
     failure...

And my words? How meaningless they seemed when all I had to do was look through the window at nature's resounding struggles. I then began feeling the familiar futility creep up my spine, this muscle telegraphing the next one that they must now turn themselves into steel wire, and ratchet the old vertebrae another notch. Fight or flee. That's what it always comes down to, when you're faced with going back to page one. Either you pick up that spear and fling it at the tiger, or...

Or what?

Or, does God really not deduct from a man's life span the hours spent fishing?

The hell with it! Let's try it and see.

Before I could possibly change my mind or be caught by the more diligent folk, I grabbed my flyrod in its aluminum case. Down in the log barn where Pete had been kicked unconscious by the colt so long before, I saddled a crooked-legged little mare that he and I had raised. Decima, we called her, after a young Irish lass John had taken a shine to, back in those days. Lately I'd been running Decima out on a lot of rides to nowhere, so she wasn't exactly pleased by the prospect. Yet, after we'd left the corral and she realized the trip couldn't be avoided, her gait quickened, as if, the sooner I get this damn fool to wherever, the sooner he'll bring me home.

When we reached the tawny hills above the ranch, I slowed her, and we rode in a quiet sort of emptiness, peopled only by ghosts. She picked her way around the first boggy spring hole, as if she were telling me, remember? That's where Johnny roped that mean white bull, and got dragged, horse and all, through the slime. Then there was the hillside of wildflowers, gone dead now of course. But the dry cow elk, the one who tried to change herself into a steer—she'd always loved that place. It was where we photographed her. And still in its tall grass lay the bones of those sickly, cheap steers, the survivors of the awful summer of Faustino. Had it not been for the miracle of slow, patient old Rex, we never would have cleaned these hills of any of them, let alone made them cross our log bridge in a storm. As we lifted higher, up a cut in the hills, Decima seemed to lead me right to the place where the Sno-Cat had spun out in that December blizzard, Teddy and I peering through the windshield with our hearts in our mouths... until we'd heard, over the throb of the engine, faint cries above us: Tom and the little Mexican boy, rolling on top of the snow toward us.

Where did they all go, those twenty years of Eliot's? The trying, failing years. Well, they were out here someplace, each one marked with sadness and joy we could never forget.

Again, the hell with it. Love it or leave it. Go fishing!

I let Decima run, her gutty crooked legs flinging out, kicking down the stalks of dead elkweed, leaping the sage. We began startling herds of antelope, sending them streaming down the hills, followed by warbling sandhill cranes that looked as brown and leggy as deer taking off. And so we ran on, until we came to the top of the world where the great Mother Mountain lay.

So she always seemed to me, looking at her all these years—loving her, this granite giant there on her back, her glittering fingers toying with the clouds. The Wind

River Range was her left leg, arched at the knee and furled with snow showers. Her right leg was the shadowed mound of the Wyoming Range. But where I seemed driven to go, this day, was into the rich darkness between, the womb of the mountains from which flowed the streams that gave us life. One of these, feeding into a tiny, almost inaccessible lake, was a treasure for those who made the effort to get there. In this lake were golden trout.

The first time I went to the lake, I was with an outfitter named Snook. No better man could you find if you wanted to catch goldens. Because these rare fish seem to know what a prize they are, they're frugal with their desires, diffident, wary. Just when you think you've learned how to hook them, they glitter away toward the depths, and you have to start all over.

But Snook knew how, and with good reason. For nearly sixty years he'd made a living out of these mountains, trapping, tracking bear and bighorn sheep. And in the late fall, after he'd done his fishing and hunting, he'd pull on his snowshoes and plod twenty miles a day to feed elk, so the herd would make it through another winter. When Snook finally wore out his hip sockets, he persuaded a surgeon to put store-bought ones in, and they don't bother his snowshoeing a bit!

As Decima and I clicked our way up through the slide and rock and neared the lake, I remembered that first afternoon with Snook. I don't know if he was testing my toughness or what, but he made us walk in. Climbing over those rocks at eleven thousand feet, I had to stop often to catch my breath. Not Snook. He just kept humping steadily over granite slabs that grew to be the size of freight cars. When we reached the lake, the clouds that obscured it had burned away. We stood in the brilliant sun, marveling at the beauty of this mountain jewel. As we set up our rods, I could almost taste the record golden that awaited me in the depths.

Now in those days, because I was just freshly arrived from the city, I was still in my "performance-casting" stage. To throw that big looping line for distance was my goal. Therefore, because the lake was ringed by some timber, I went around it to a large rock that jutted out and would thus give me ample room for my super backcasts.

I was still then stranger enough to Snook that I asked if maybe he wanted this rock himself. Nope, he said, and grinned. Then he hunched off like an old, used turtle and perched on a tiny rock, in the shade. His "fly," self-tied, resembled no known living organism. It was simply a hunk of orange wool he'd taken from his wife's sweater. "When that there sweater plays out," he'd told me on the trip up, "reckon I'll have to quit fishin'."

I glanced across the lake at Snook when he made his first "cast." It was a writhe that splatted out the fly no more than fifteen feet in front of him. I thought, surely he'd cast again to get some acceptable distance, or at least give the fly a few twitches. But it remained motionless. Snook was sitting in a heap, dozing.

I, meanwhile, was shooting out beautiful looping coils of line, my fly alighting as gently as a mosquito, and when it wouldn't work in one place, I'd whip it up and try another. I covered acres of that deep, cold water, twitching, luring. I was so busy casting that I almost didn't hear a faint croak, like a frog.

"Agin." That was all.

When I traced the sound to Snook, I saw him hunched down in the weeds. "Again, what?" I hollered.

Snook held up a golden trout of perhaps two pounds.

Agin-agin-agin. That was the only sound on the lake, his maddening croak when he'd pull out the next fish. We ended the afternoon with Snook's splat-and-doze technique netting him six beauties, and my lashing and gnashing exactly zero.

Well, what was it? Witchcraft? Had he hypnotized those fish?

Back then, on that first trip, I didn't know the answer. But now, as Decima and I finally arrived at the lake— when I looked at that glittering water, I felt I could see in it what Snook had. I left Decima to graze, and I walked around, not to my grand rock anymore, but to Snook's little one. Sitting down with my back against it, in the tall warm grass, I clasped my forearms around my legs, and for an uncounted time just waited, as Snook had.

Because now, dimly, I could begin to understand what that waiting meant: the waiting without hope. In Snook's waiting he seemed to have linked himself with the rhythm of all living things. He didn't threaten nature. He was simply part of it. And thus, to him, the goldens had responded by lifting themselves slowly out of the pro- tected depths until that hideous hunk of orange yarn transformed itself into something that belonged in their world.

And my world now? Well, fish, man! I had come all this way, all these twenty years to catch the damn golden, hadn't I? Get at it, fish! Too soon, it would be time to go home.

I took my flybox out of my vest, opened it, and set it in the grass. Yet somehow—maybe the fatigue of the long trip up there—I didn't want to have to begin to "catch" again. A few mosquitoes began to buzz around me, and then grasshoppers flickered away in the grass, as if, in the unaccustomed warmth, they weren't prepared to accept that summer had really died. I began studying the glassy dark of the lake. No, nothing was working. No rises. I lit my pipe and began to watch a little more.

There was a faint ripple of wind, whorling the water. A *diablito* ("dust devil") we used to call them in Arizona. But this wasn't Arizona. Where were we? I wondered. Where was I, right at that moment, and was it all the same?

But then as my eyes wandered, following the whisper devil of wind, it spun its way to the far end of the lake.

Here, the sun gleamed on water I hadn't noticed that first time with Snook. I squinted so I could see it better.

Cutting down out of rocks through willows and clumps of miners' lettuce was a narrow stream. Clearly, it was the source of the golden lake. But now, sometime in the years since I'd visited here, beaver had come in and, from the edge of the lake back upward, constructed a series of pools. I could see the gleaming log dams marking each one. It was these beaver ponds that the sun was catching, and turning gold.

If the goldens spawned in the creek, I thought, then they'd be easier to catch there. So go over and fish, I told myself. Walk from one pool to the next, like stepping-stones that were the years on this trail.

And fish with what? What kind of flies? As I looked down at my flybox, all I could see was a disarray of hackles, furs, deer hairs. Old flies, the same shabby equipment I seemed to have been fishing with all my life. Many of the patterns I'd even brought with me from the cities I'd left behind.

But did they still work, for the man I hoped I was now? Snook had used just orange yarn from his wife's sweater. But what could I use, from Teddy, from Tom, John, Pete—all the friends of these years? Had they taught me any kind of fly, for the golden pools?

Well, old Rex had. With him, his fly would be, what? Maybe a snail? The slowest thing in the world. I could imagine it in my fingers as I tied it on my leader. "Jest slow—slowin' 'em." Enjoying every one of those twenty-four hours that God made us.

And maybe, after the first snail of a fly in the first pool, I'd walk up to the next one, and slowing, slowly I'd be hearing something new, wouldn't I? Like Chisty in Arizona, "hearing" that calf. If the ear was the secret, perhaps I'd use a hare's ear, because all it heard was "Who? Who? Who?" Who are you now? Who are you uniquely intended to be?

A ridiculous exercise! I found myself thinking. How did I even know there were goldens in those tiny ponds? I squinted again toward them, but the water was too brilliant, refracting in the sun. If I could only "see" into that third pool, then I might have faith that something was there, beneath the surface. But what fly to see? An Eye of some kind? How would I make it, out of what? My fingers trembled as I fumbled through my old flies, old materials. I was indeed trembling like the tall, stooped padre down in Sasabe on his last night. Yet the poor people of that poor world had an eye to see beyond him, didn't they? They saw their golden beneath his surface.

By now I was spilling the flies out into my palm. One big muddler, streamed in marabou, was crusted in silver. It gleamed like a silver dollar, luring me to spend it, and judging me if I failed. No golden would ever rise to such a fraud, so throw it away, grind it with my heel into the wet grass, so it would hook no other fisherman as it had hooked me.

But then what, what fly for the next pool, the next step up? Because if I hadn't caught the golden by this time, I'd begin to fear that I never would. So, put fear on my line and fling it roaring through the air. Grizzly—make it out of grizzly hair, let it thunder until all the fears lurking in the shadows were gone.

Yet still did I fear. Suppose there was a storm on the way home? A lightning bolt, or Decima would fall into a badger hole? And I, wasting precious time, dawdling over an allegory that could never be! So escape it then! Rush up to the next pool, tie on a Silverwing, that was it! The wing of a jet, to send me fleeing out of this hopeless struggle. Escape, as Red and I had tried that day on the desert. Get back to the important things.

But what were they? Did they lie in the next, still larger pool? If I caught a golden here, would I leap in, as my old friend had, and seize it with my bare hands? Hold it up to

be photographed with a sadness in my smile? So make this
fly into the deception it was. Shape it out of bread dough,
in the form of the Human Loins. So that when it struck
the water and the golden saw it, he could watch its desire
melt away, before he had the urge to give his life for it.

But still more pools to be tried. One for old Clance.
Make his fly the Hermit Crab, lonely, but not alone. And
follow it in the next pool by the Gnat, so small by now that
the golden might finally believe this was an authentic
creature.

And on the final two pools, just two left—if the patterns
had not worked thus far, would they work here? But if I
didn't keep trying I'd never know, and maybe not then.
Because the first of these pools was so narrow and weed-
grown, it was a chore to fish, the hardest challenge. But if I
had to accept this to catch the golden, shouldn't I welcome
it? Do it! Put on a fly that could cut through the nuisance
and the sacrifice, the fights, the failures, the machos, and
the amors. Accept their challenge with a Sword.

And when it had slashed, and lost, and slashed again,
still not rewarded, move finally to the last pool. The
biggest one of all, and its curving shape indicated the only
fly the golden would ever take here.

A fly in the shape of a Heart!

Fished with love. But a new kind now. A love that cared
very much about all the long struggle up through the
ponds; a love that fished with the greatest skill and
dedication the fisherman could give it.

And then—this was the surmounting—a love that did
not care for the reward. Whether he caught the golden or
not.

Because, just in trying all these pools, perhaps he
already had.

That's why I didn't even fish that afternoon. No, just sat
there by Snook's rock, remembering again: "But perhaps
it's neither gain nor loss. For us, there is only the trying.
The rest is not our business."

I carried it with me, that line, on the trail down from the golden pools. There was an old friend I'd known, a man I left behind me in my old life. I thought that now, finally, it seemed time for me to drop him a note, and tell him how it is out here.

God knows, he might even get to like it.

6

Ending the Beginning

But the dream never ends.

That's the tantalizing quality of it. No one is ever quite there. Yet the blessedness is the hope that you could be. And so you seize the moment with gratitude for the gift it is.

Dawn now, the stillness of the world. That's when I feel it with the greatest joy, that instant of liberation when the corrals of the California ranch are still dark. But the hills beyond, the skyline of live oaks and digger pines, are just being rubbed by a pinkish gold.

It's another ride, this day, not the last I hope, not the first, simply a captured instant in the mundane cycling of life on the ranch. Before it gets too hot, we have to ride over the skyline and round up cattle in a valley just beyond.

It's a family affair as usual, Pete in the lead and enjoying ordering Teddy and me around. Rita is with him, having just left Tess and little Joe asleep in the Volkswagen bus, parked under the willow beside our house. When the kids wake up, they won't be frightened. They know it's roundup today, and they'll drift sleepy-eyed into our kitchen and fix themselves cereal.

I saddle my thoroughbred stallion Baboquivari for myself, and for Teddy, a wild-eyed little Mexican horse named Moro. They've both come from the hard rocks in Arizona, the old life there. I named Babo for the sacred peak of the Papago Indians that towered above the Las Delicias. I'd hoped to race him, but when he was only a week old, a mountain lion came prowling around his corral. In panic, Babo rammed the fence and lost an eye. I did try him at the races because he had the blood and a noble heart, but after watching the rival jockeys slamming into his blind side, I finally just brought him home, to breed our mares and take me to the tops of the mountains.

"So come on, Bob," I say, and he leaps out with a snort, following the other horses up a dewy track into the green hills. Now, with the sun slanting through the lace of wild oats, I can't believe the richness of this land. The spring rains have soaked us for weeks now. I can smell the earth growing, the tiny buds on the oaks. All around us are carpets of blue and yellow flowers, and the sea breeze from the Pacific carries with it not only a cool saltiness, but a buzzing of unseen bees.

The land of milk and honey, the blessing that we should find ourselves here—yes, at this moment I almost want to cry out at the wonder of it. But there's always a reality too. Pete has reined in ahead of me. He has a time consciousness, even if I don't right now. "Dammit, Fred," he glowers at his mother, who has dismounted and is walking Moro, "don't baby that ornery little runt. You'll wear out long before he does."

But I doubt that, as I glance over at Teddy, young and Yoga-honed in litheness, and, most important, still with a contentment in her eyes. As many times as we've moved cattle together and regardless of the steepness of the trails, she's never tired of it. Indeed, she always insists on dismounting at various times and "resting" the poor old so-and-so of the moment. So now she just laughs at Pete and keeps right on walking. "I tell you," he says, "this valley is rough to gather when it gets hot. We've got to patch out."

Or do we, I wonder, and what for? Well yes, the young man's ego wants to do things right. But for the old bird in Levi's, sack of bones and a thatch of gray hair pressed down under a wetback's straw sombrero—does it really matter when we get home? Because around us now the world is exploding with life. On the higher slopes, I hear clickings in the dark chamiso underbrush. Those are bound to be the Mud Springs covey of quail I've been trying to find for so long. But I don't quite see them because Rita's crying out, her gold hair flashing in the sun: "Pete, look. Porkchops!"

Out of the chamiso comes a squealing rumbling family of wild boars. The father is a hairy black Russian with vicious tusks. The sow has the belt of a Poland China crossbred around her slogging belly. But it's the piglets that we have to laugh at. They're tiny and rusty red, as identical as cocktail sausages popped out of a can. Once Pete had captured one and given it to his kids to put in a cage. He told them it was just a regular pig, so Tess simply named him "Regular."

As in mundane, taken for granted. Yet how can I take this for granted, without thanks? To rise finally to the skyline and see the sweep of the green valley below, cut with the silver glinting of flowing streams. By now in the climb, our horses are tired, so we catch a breath in the shade of an oak. Pete gives us the game plan, pointing down into the next valley: Teddy will ride the left slopes, Rita the right. Pete will cover the reddish arroyo in the center, actually a gorge, out of which we'll begin to push the cows uphill. It will be like pouring water uphill, but Teddy and Rita are laughing in the challenge. Their voices trail across the slope and I lose sight of them. Well, yes, Peter has told me where I should ride, but for a moment I want to delay, just to sit there patting Babo's neck, and to look down at how far we've come. Babo tried to be a racehorse, but had a blind spot. And me? Trying to be a writer and rancher, and who the devil knew, nor did it matter anymore.

Yet, at exactly that moment, in my smug sense of confidence, I happen to glance down the slope. Something is there that shouldn't be. It's in the wrong pasture, a dark shiny creature slowly edging into the sun. Then brazenly, as if she knows I'm watching her, she looks directly up at me.

"You damned tramp!" I cry. That's exactly what she is, this spackle-faced Brahma cow that for years now has managed to madden and beat us. She won't stay put! That's her problem. Restless devil, just when we've pushed her into the herd where she belongs, she'll jump the fence and trot boldly out into some other pasture that must look greener to her.

As I start to curse her—how can we ever get you bred if you keep jumping?—at that moment, suddenly I have to smile. Look closer to home, old boy. What about all the fences you've jumped?

What about the moose that my foreman, John Fandek, photographed in Wyoming, leaping to some greener pasture? The moose, the Brahma cow, myself—all of us trying to find it on the other side. So, there's an instant of doubt. I look down and see far below a gleaming slab of concrete: the house that John and Nancy have designed for us. Roots, responsibility on the build. And, yes, who wouldn't be happy, now, here, in this exuberant morning? But if that old demon still can't be put down, if it still keeps driving me to want to jump the next fence, then what? Has the beginning of the dream ended at all?

Maybe my boys don't think so. I keep hearing Pete, not long before, when he was terrifying his mother: "Listen, I know Big O. Once he shoots enough quail, he'll begin to go stir-crazy back in these hills. You'll never keep him here." And John, wryly, trying to make me guarantee that this would be my last and final house. Even Tom, long distance from New York, had said: "It's probably a good thing you're back in California, Dad. And I don't mean the ranch part of it. What you'll have to do now is get back into the action, mix it up in L.A. Any writer has to hone himself on the hard realities, the studios, all the rat race you hate..."

Suddenly I realized that what I'm hating most right now is that black devil cow—personification of all the fence jumpers, and my inability to slay her once and for all. Well, this is the time. Teach her a lesson, gallop down and whip her back into the pasture where she belongs.

But the moment I flick the reins up on Babo, to start after her, his head twists to the opposite side the slope. Even though it's to his left, his blind eye, he's "seen" something here, caught some rhythm I'm unaware of. He trembles, then snorts toward the valley where my family of riders has gone.

I hear it at first, a rattling of hooves, then I see it. Thousands of feet below, a gray streak is racing toward me. It's Moro, running wildly, something wrong! His chest is streaked with blood, the stirrups flailing, thumping his sweating flanks.

Teddy is off and gone.

Fear clutches me for a rigid, useless instant. Where is she? What's happened? We all know the risk. Have a horse wreck in these hills, off by yourself at the bottom of some hidden canyon, it would take a helicopter to get you out—if they could even find you in the first place.

"Bob!" I cry, and he seems to understand. He leaps off the skyline, flattening into a run. We careen through an oak thicket, dodging, jumping fallen branches as I pursue Moro.

But he's a tough little nut, raised in the rocks near Sasabe, and crazed with fear now. He turns, darting, trying to outrun Babo down an arroyo that isn't like any racetrack. It's a perilous place, downed timber, deep gashes, gullies cut blood red in the earth. I keep think-ing—and nothing makes sense in a moment like this—if I can somehow catch this little loco, maybe he'll lead me to Teddy.

We twist and thunder back and forth like polo ponies after a ball. Like old Red, the day the cow butted Teddy. But thank God it's Babo now, a young horse with the heart in him to go for the roses. At last, by the fence, we run Moro down. His flanks are badly cut, his eyes red with terror. As I seize his reins, I want to shout at him, Where is she? What did you do with her?

Then, jerking him along with me, I hurry lower to the valley floor. Search the tall grass, brushpiles, crumbling arroyos. She could be lying anywhere here. And then what? Unconscious, broken bones? I shout for her, my voice echoing away on the wind. The old reflex is to expect the worst, to want to control it.

But Babo doesn't know of such things. Not the past. He is where he is. And so, almost imperceptibly, his ears flicker. We're not alone here.

I twist in the saddle, hearing it first, the shoe-clicking of a tired horse. Down a long slope of wild oats comes Rita's

big horse, Six, a glistening roan with flecks of sweat on
him. Atop him, Rita has doubled in size. Clinging to her,
swaying behind her saddle, is Teddy. They're both
laughing in the sunlight.

Laughing, damn them!

I'm trying to shout: "Do you know how long I've been
hunting you, what I've been thinking!"

Teddy is dismounting, smears of mud on her face and
shirt, but smiling. "You went off!" I cry.

"Oh, not really." And then she's saying, "Poor little
Moro," and stroking the bloody cuts on his chest.

"What happened," Rita says, "we were working a
sidehill in the tall grass. Moro couldn't see it, neither
could Fred. There was some old barbed wire. When Moro
got into it, he freaked, and Fred had to leave."

"Dammit!" I cry. "Couldn't you have held onto the
reins so he wouldn't be running around here empty, and
scaring hell out of everybody!"

"Oh, we weren't scared," Teddy answers, mounting
again. "It was just that damn wire."

A homesteader's wire, that's what it was, curled and left
to rust on the slope where his old dream had gone down.

And yet, he had stayed there, hadn't he? He'd come to
stay, and dug it out in the oaks and digger pines for as
many years as God had given him.

And what of me? Will I be staying here too? Isn't this
finally as much of the dream as one ever gets in this world?

Yes, I think, there'll be rides to the golden pools and
chases of the devils too, all part of the ending beginning
that says only: there's no going back anymore. Wasn't
that the dream, not to?

So we start down to the ranch, herding the few cows and
calves we've collected. Our cottage industry, the poor
man's foxhunt. And midway on the trail I catch a glimpse
of the fence-jumper cow, leering at us from her hillside of
brush.

Teddy also sees her. "Well, what do you think?" I ask. "Shall I put her back in where she belongs?"

Teddy smiles and says she is where she belongs.

Then Peter jogs up beside us. "Quit woolgathering, will you? We've got to get these baby calves to the field where they can mother up."

"Relax," I tell him. "We're almost there." And still and still moving, we keep riding down the long green hills, to home.

Whoever looks for God has found Him

PASCAL